American Exceptionalism in a New Era

American Exceptionalism in a New Era

Rebuilding the Foundation of Freedom and Prosperity

EDITED BY THOMAS W. GILLIGAN

HOOVER INSTITUTION PRESS

STANFORD UNIVERSITY   STANFORD, CALIFORNIA

With its eminent scholars and world-renowned library and archives, the Hoover Institution seeks to improve the human condition by advancing ideas that promote economic opportunity and prosperity, while securing and safeguarding peace for America and all mankind. The views expressed in its publications are entirely those of the authors and do not necessarily reflect the views of the staff, officers, or Board of Overseers of the Hoover Institution.

www.hoover.org

Hoover Institution Press Publication No. 686

Hoover Institution at Leland Stanford Junior University, Stanford, California 94305-6003

First printing 2017

23 22 21 20 19 18 17   7 6 5 4 3 2 1

Manufactured in the United States of America

The paper used in this publication meets the minimum Requirements of the American National Standard for Information Sciences—Permanence of Paper for Printed Library Materials, ANSI/NISO Z39.48-1992. ∞

Cataloging-in-Publication Data is available from the Library of Congress.

ISBN: 978-0-8179-2124-8 (cloth. : alk. paper)
ISBN: 978-0-8179-2126-2 (epub)
ISBN: 978-0-8179-2127-9 (mobi)
ISBN: 978-0-8179-2128-6 (PDF)

CONTENTS

Contents

FOREWORD

Twice a year, the Hoover Institution hosts a retreat for its supporters and benefactors. The purpose of these retreats is to showcase the vivid range of intellectual expertise and flair within the Hoover fellowship. The presentations and discussions that comprise these retreats reflect Hoover's mission, which is to generate policy ideas that promote prosperity, peace, and liberty in America and the wider world.

Hoover is the home of *ideas defining a free society;* many of these concepts are introduced at our semiannual retreats. The retreat in the fall of 2016 was organized around the topic of American exceptionalism. To be sure, the meaning and implications of American exceptionalism can elicit spirited debate and controversy, particularly if the concept is understood to imply superiority and preeminence. But at the most elemental level, three questions are central to this idea and how it relates to contemporary public policy.

First, is America different from other nations in ways that are good or preferable? For example, is the American economy more vibrant or dynamic? Is the pace of innovation or diffusion of new technologies more rapid than in other countries? Is labor mobility greater and economic opportunity more meaningful to people, particularly the young, in America than in other nations? Is America's political system more responsive, representative, deliberative, and democratic than those found elsewhere? Are America's educational institutions and civic culture more conducive to producing a population fit for democratic self-governance? Many of the essays contained in this volume confirm that, indeed, America is exceptional in these significant ways.

Second, what are the sources of American exceptionalism? How important is America's unique history—the settling of the New World—to its desirable attributes? Do America's ethnic diversity and history with immigration play a crucial role in its positive distinctiveness? What part do America's constitutional and legal systems play in fostering the dynamism of the American political and economic culture? Are its governing policies and organizational principles responsible for its differential success among the nations of the world? Several of the essays contained in this volume attempt to pinpoint some of the key causal factors for American exceptionalism.

Third, and most sensitive, is American exceptionalism in decline? Is America now, more than ever, just like other countries around the world? Is the performance of the American economy—its growth and productivity rates, its pace of technological innovation, and its provision of meaningful economic opportunity for broad swaths of its people—regressing toward the global mean? Is America's leadership in sustaining the postwar liberal international order—encompassing peace, democracy, liberty, and prosperity—being assumed by other nations with decidedly different values and goals? Is America, in fact, in retreat? The essays in this volume provide some stimulating, and generally positive, answers to these provocative questions.

Discussions of American exceptionalism are central to America's identity and role in the world and, therefore, essential for the formation of contemporary public policy, both foreign and domestic. This Hoover volume contributes to the critical conversation in varied and valuable ways. I am certain that you will enjoy these readings and hope that they will stimulate your thinking about the distinctive nature of the American experiment and the productive roles that America can play in the world.

Our thanks to the many individuals who assisted with this volume, beginning with the Hoover Institution's supporters, whose generosity and engagement made the 2016 fall retreat possible and whose contributions underlie the entirety of the institution's work. We also thank Denise Elson for helping organize the conference program on which this volume is based, as well as Mary Gingell and her team for seamlessly executing that event. For developing the conference proceedings into a cohesive publication, we thank Tunku Varadarajan, Christopher Dauer, and Kyle Palermo, as well as Barbara Arellano and her team at the Hoover Institution Press.

—Thomas W. Gilligan

PART ONE

Foundations of American Exceptionalism

Is America Still the "Hope of Earth"?

Origins and Underpinnings of American Exceptionalism

PAUL E. PETERSON

Advocates of American exceptionalism say the United States is special, a nation for the world to admire, a country worthy of emulation, a place chosen for destiny. Their claim resembles the assumption made by the young child at a Jewish seder who asks, "Why is this night different from all other nights?" But is it really correct to say that America is exceptional?

Without doubt, the United States differs from other countries in the same way the air, stars, and smells vary from one night to another. Barack Obama put it this way: "I believe in American exceptionalism . . . just as I suspect the Brits believe in British exceptionalism . . . and the Greeks believe in Greek exceptionalism."[1] All countries can find something to brag about. Vladimir Putin thinks it is pernicious to say anything beyond that. He warns, "It is extremely dangerous to encourage people to think of themselves as exceptional." He is quick to agree that "there are big countries, and small countries, rich and poor, those with long democratic traditions, and those still finding their way to democracy." But, he says, "we must not forget that God created us equal."[2]

Abraham Lincoln thought otherwise. Like the innocent child at a seder, he had no reservations about American exceptionalism. The Declaration of Independence, he said, "gave liberty, not alone to the people of this country, but hope to the world for all future time."[3] If the American democracy collapsed, the negative impacts for democracy would be global. If the Union split into two nations, European monarchs would rejoice at the division. When searching for meaning in the midst of the tragedy of the Civil War, he invariably returned to his belief that the United States "shall nobly save or meanly lose the last best hope of earth."[4] The president was not certain whether the great American experiment would survive. For him it remained a question whether "a new nation conceived in liberty . . . can long endure."[5]

Tocqueville's Theory

Lincoln's thinking about American exceptionalism was likely shaped by Alexis de Tocqueville.[6] The French aristocrat, writing in the post-Napoleonic period, expected democracies to transform themselves into dictatorships. People continuously ask their governments to make improvements, he said. To meet expectations, leaders centralize power so they can implement reform on a national scale. Local institutions crumble, and the people's capacity for self-government erodes. Centralization breeds tyranny.[7]

Tocqueville sailed to the United States during the 1830s to see whether his new nation refuted this theory. He traveled broadly and inquired widely into every facet of American life, then blended his observations together into a powerful explanation of the country's exceptional capacity for sustaining democracy. Here is what he concluded:

> The situation of the Americans is entirely exceptional, and it may be believed that no democratic people will ever be put in the same situation. Their entirely Puritan origin, their uniquely commercial habits, even the country that they inhabit . . . had to concentrate the American mind in a singular way in the concern for purely material things. The passions, needs, education, circumstances, everything seems in fact to combine to bend the inhabitant of the United States toward the earth. Religion alone makes him, from time to time, turn a fleeting and distracted gaze toward heaven. So let us stop seeing all democratic nations with the face of the American people, and let us try finally to consider them with their own features.[8]

The strong state and local governments of the "country they inhabit" encouraged a practical focus on solving problems at the community level. "Their exclusively commercial habits" closed their minds to grand political schemes to reform and transform society. "Their strictly Puritanical origin" focused their attention on self-reliance, hard work, and enough learning to allow them to read the Bible. "Passions" and "wants" drew the citizen of the United States "earthward," toward simple, home-grown solutions rather than pie-in-the-sky schemes for societal salvation being peddled in Europe.

What is exceptional about the United States, then, is its capacity to preserve liberty within a democracy. When the colonies separated from Great Britain, Congress issued a Declaration of Independence that asserted the "unalienable right" to "life, liberty and the pursuit of happiness." Legitimate governments "secure these rights" and "derive their just powers from the consent of the governed." The citizen, not the collectivity, was placed at the center of the political system. Liberty was given priority over social guarantees. Opportunity was available to all if only they would do the hard work and develop the entrepreneurial skill to acquire it. Howard University scholar Ralph Bunche put it well:

> Every man in the street, white, black, red or yellow, knows that this is "the land of the free," the "land of opportunity," the "cradle of liberty," the "home of democracy," that the American flag symbolizes the "equality of all men" and guarantees to us all "the protection of life, liberty and property," freedom of speech, freedom of religion and racial tolerance.[9]

But what sustains this creed? How did the United States escape liberty-depriving centralization? Why did the country defy Tocqueville's law? Will it continue to do so throughout the twenty-first century?

Explaining the Exception

Picking up Tocqueville's baton, scholars have identified seven factors that have contributed to the exceptional success of American democracy: (1) absence of feudal institutions; (2) early, widespread political participation; (3) federalism and divided government; (4) rapid economic growth; (5) the frontier; (6) widespread education; and (7) continuous immigration.

Absence of feudal institutions

First and foremost, the United States was a new nation that had no feudal heritage.[10] When American patriots dethroned George III, the colonial aristocracy was run out of town on a rail. Nor did the United States have a national church. No Westminster Abbey has ever stood next to the nation's capital. The religious groups dominant in a number of colonies—Anglicans in Virginia, Puritans in New England, Quakers in Pennsylvania—lost their special status within a decade or two after the Revolution. None of them had a chance of becoming the religion of the new nation. American clergy could not pander for subsidies from the government. They had to persuade their parishioners to give generously.

Early, widespread political participation

Without noblemen and clergy fighting to protect their privileges, colonial barriers to widespread citizen participation disappeared quickly, a second factor that contributed to this exceptional experiment in democracy. By 1820 white male suffrage was universal in nearly all states. Shortly thereafter, Andrew Jackson rallied frontiersmen, swept the Virginia dynasty from power, and instituted a "spoils system" that allocated government jobs to party loyalists. In ensuing years political machines mobilized the electorate so effectively that the turnout rate in presidential elections among eligible voters ran higher in 1844 and 1848 than it has in the twenty-first century (figure 1).

Machine politicians, though ready to take advantage of the opportunities available to them, never challenged the political order. Because they were well entrenched, socialist political parties and radical trade unions, such as the Industrial Workers of the World ("Wobblies"), could make few inroads. The politically engaged focused on the spoils of office rather than on Marxist schemes to nationalize the means of production. Socialist Eugene Debs managed to capture 6 percent of the presidential vote in 1912, but that turned out to be the party's high-water mark in the United States.[11] As Tocqueville expected, the American working class remained pragmatic, their eyes focused "earthward."

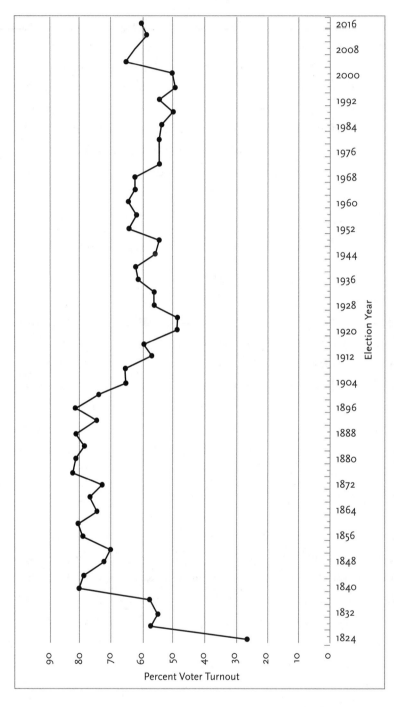

Figure 1. A Higher Percentage of White Males Voted in 1844 Than in 2008.

Federalism and divided government

Politics remained local because the Constitution divided power between the state and national governments. In Tocqueville's day, the federal role was limited to setting tariffs, selling land, and running a post office. All other services—police, fire, sanitation, schools, and so forth—were provided by state and local governments. Even today, over a third of all domestic governmental expenditure is paid for out of taxes raised by state and local governments. The federal government pays for national defense, Social Security, Medicare, and other welfare services, but most of the rest remains a state and local responsibility. As much as we have centralized power in the United States, the lower tiers remain vital components of our governmental system.

The sharing of power between Congress and the executive, and the further division of power between House and Senate, slows down the rate of policy change and moderates the policies that are designed. At a time when many European countries were creating their welfare states by providing old-age pensions, long-term unemployment benefits, health care for all, and a tuition-free college education, divided power within the United States stalled the process of change and forced the adoption of more limited interventions. Not until the Great Depression of the 1930s did the New Deal begin to create the alphabet soup of agencies that formed the welfare state, and the programs then established did not come to full fruition until Medicare and Medicaid were signed into law by the Lyndon Johnson administration and the Affordable Care Act was enacted during the Barack Obama administration. In higher education, the Europeans offered students free tuition, while the United States set up loan programs. Europeans like to report that they have free medicine, free education, and ample benefits for the unemployed. But the taxpayer pays heavily for these "free gifts." As compared to the 26 percent of the gross domestic product (GDP) paid in taxes in the United States, well over 30 percent of GDP in Germany and the United

Kingdom and over 40 percent of GDP in France, Italy, Denmark, and Sweden is being collected by the government.

These international differences are quite consistent with the state of public opinion on the two sides of the Atlantic. Americans expect individuals to work hard and solve economic problems on their own or with the help of their families. Europeans are more ready to turn to the government for a solution. A World Values survey found that "less than 30% of Americans believe that the poor are trapped in poverty while 60% of Europeans have this belief."[12] Nearly 70 percent of Americans tell pollsters that they think they have the free choice and control over their lives to get ahead. Only about 50 percent of German and British citizens feel the same way, and the percentages are around 35 percent in France and Italy.[13] Should we rely on the government to reduce income inequality? A majority of Americans don't think so. Only 30 percent of Americans say yes, as compared to about 80 percent of the Spanish and approximately 60 percent of the Germans and the British.[14]

In 2016 respondents in several countries were asked if "lack of effort on his or her own part" is the most important reason for a person being poor. Forty-six percent of Americans said that was the case, but only 37 percent of UK respondents offered the same response. In France, that percentage fell to 23 percent, and in Italy it was just 14 percent. Americans said the tax rate on the top 1 percent of taxpayers should be 25 percent, while the British would put it at 37 percent, the French at 44 percent, and the Italians at 38 percent.[15] Especially interesting is the finding that "in Europe, the happiness of the poor is strongly negatively affected by inequality," while the happiness of the poor in the United States seems to be "totally unaffected by inequality."[16]

Rapid economic growth

The "earthward" focus of the American public has been reinforced by a large, integrated, fast-growing, high-wage economy, the fourth factor that contributes to American exceptionalism. Even during the colonial period, labor was scarce and wages ran higher than in England.[17] As soon as independence was secured, the new nation put into place the fundamentals that would ensure sustained economic progress. The country kept common-law property protections inherited from Britain. The US land survey ordered by Congress at Thomas Jefferson's instigation divided the country into rectangles with the exactitude needed to define precisely the property to be secured. The Constitution eliminated tariff barriers among the states. With property rights safe and the ability to sell products on a continental scale, entrepreneurs had strong incentives to innovate and expand. The US economy grew so rapidly that it surpassed Britain's by 1890 and dominated the world economy throughout the twentieth century.

The frontier

This economic growth generated westward expansion, which had its own impact on American political culture. The frontier hypothesis presented by Henry Turner Jackson before his fellow historians at the 1893 World's Columbian Exposition in Chicago explains the connection with American exceptionalism in these terms:

> This perennial rebirth, this fluidity of American life, this expansion westward with its new opportunities, its continuous touch with the simplicity of primitive society, furnish the forces dominating American character. . . .
>
> The frontier is productive of individualism. . . . It produces antipathy to control, and particularly to any direct control. The tax-gatherer is viewed as a representative of oppression.[18]

Lincoln understood the importance of the frontier to the American experiment. He knew railroads opened the door to economic prosperity, so he, as a lawyer, ably defended them against provincial interests that tried to stop them from laying down their tracks and building their bridges. As president, he facilitated the expansion of the transcontinental railroad so that it was only four years after his assassination when the Golden Spike driven into the plains of Utah united East with West. Lincoln also signed the Homestead Act, which gave 160 acres of land to anyone who would plow the fields. Notably, the law gave away federal property only to those willing to sweat and toil to make it productive.

Widespread education

The frontier explanation for American exceptionalism is well known. The sixth factor, local control of the nation's schools, is less well understood, though Tocqueville mentions schools briefly: "I do not think that in the most enlightened rural district of France, there is an intellectual movement, either so rapid, or on such scale, as in this wilderness."[19] He attributed this not to strong governmental action but to the associations "Americans make . . . [to] found hospitals, prisons, and schools."[20]

The beginnings of schools in America owe much to the influence of Puritans, who believed that children must be able to read if they are to learn the biblical truths that mark the road to salvation. They built seminaries at Harvard and Yale to train ministers who could spread the gospel into the country's interior. But it was not long before schooling was valued for secular purposes as well. Small towns learned that if they did not build schools their communities would not attract newcomers.[21] By 1870, 78 percent of school-age children were in school, as compared to just 61 percent in England.[22] Control was at the local level. In 1925 there were 130,000 school districts, many of them with just one school. "These relatively small, fiscally independent school districts," economist Claudia Goldin has pointed out, "competed with one another to attract residents." The towns and cities of America were educating children in ways consistent with local community values while Europeans were debating in national parliaments and assemblies whether schools should be sectarian or secular.

Continuous immigration

Last but not least, America was open to newcomers. Most immigrants took great risks by first crossing an ocean and then traversing a wide continent until they could find the opportunities they sought. Recently, a friend told me a family story that undoubtedly has millions of repetitions, each with its own special twist. Her great-grandmother crossed the Atlantic with her five children in 1850 without her husband, who could not leave until he paid the twenty dollars to settle a last-minute claim filed on the eve of their departure. Since the family had used all its assets to pay for the passage, the mother went ahead on her own, losing her baby en route. Her husband arrived some weeks later, and a prosperous Iowa settlement was eventually established. What kind of people would take such risks? My colleagues and I summarized the research literature on this topic as follows:

> The people who immigrated already were . . . unusually individualistic. They were more motivated to break free from the tradition of their communities. They were more ambitious, more willing to run risks in the hope of bettering themselves.
>
> Given this independent spirit, immigration and the diversity it produced never were a threat to American values. On the contrary, successive waves of immigrants rejuvenated those values. . . . There is no reason to believe that today's immigrants are any different. They, too, have left homes and families. . . . Such people display a kind of individual initiative that can rightly be considered "American," regardless of their nationality.[23]

When these risk-takers arrived in the United States, American institutions were well suited to absorbing them into the larger society. As economist Jacob Vigdor puts it,

> [American] institutions—the predominance of the English language, support of basic capitalist economic principles, and the American system of Federal government—[are] quite resilient. . . . Evidence does not support the notion that [the latest] wave of migration poses a true threat to the institutions that withstood those earlier waves. Basic indicators of assimilation, from naturalization to English ability, are if anything stronger now than they were a century ago.[24]

In short, immigration, if legal, reinforces the culture of American exceptionalism because the institutions that sustain that culture facilitate the assimilation of the newcomer.

Slavery and Exceptionalism

Slavery is the exception to the American ideals encapsulated within the concept of exceptionalism, as Tocqueville himself admitted. The Frenchman's discussion is at once painful, agonizing, enlightening, confusing, and disappointing. One can only cringe when he characterizes "Negroes" as subhuman, but one is relieved to discover he does not attribute this condition to any innate qualities but rather to the violence, persecution, and inhumanity the slaves suffered. He contrasts the energy of the farmers of the North with the lassitude of the Southern plantation. He says the slave system hurt white masters nearly as much as it harmed those they enslaved. He says freed blacks in the North were treated worse than Southern slaves. He emphasizes slavery's destructive impact on family life. Much of what he said still carries weight, but unfortunately, Tocqueville cannot find a solution that fits within the American creed.

Lincoln does better by suggesting that the price of slavery was being paid by a civil war consuming "all the wealth piled by the bondsman's two hundred and fifty years of unrequited toil" and "every drop of blood drawn with the lash" was being "paid by another drawn with the sword." But even this expectation was proven wrong. Racial progress came very slowly in the century following the day swords drew their last drops of blood. Blacks remained tied to the land as sharecroppers; their children were forced to attend low-quality, segregated elementary schools; their access to public facilities was available only on a segregated basis; and their vote was denied in Democratic primaries. African-Americans found new opportunities in the North during World War I and after the passage of the Naturalization Act of 1920. But as Gunnar Myrdal described in *The American Dilemma,* a classic study of race relations on the eve of World War II, US racial practices remained in sharp contradiction to its creedal commitment to liberty and equality of opportunity.[25]

The civil rights movement ameliorated Myrdal's dilemma. A growing black middle class entered the professions, the public sector, and the news and entertainment industries. Ralph Bunche was recognized for his scholarly achievements with an appointment as a United Nations undersecretary; Jackie Robinson emerged as a baseball hero; Marian Anderson sang at Constitutional Hall; psychologist Kenneth Clark informed the *Brown* decision; Leontyne Price brought down the Metropolitan Opera house; Edward Brooke was chosen by Massachusetts voters to be their senator; Gwen Ifill anchored public television's six o'clock news show; and, eventually, Barack Obama was elected president of the United States. But despite these and tens of thousands of other individual accomplishments, slavery's legacy has not been erased. In 2015 nearly a quarter of African-American families were living in poverty (as compared to less than 10 percent of white families).[26] The percentage of children living with an unmarried mother increased from 20 percent to 50 percent between 1960 and 2013 (as compared to an increase from 7 percent to 19 percent among whites over the same time period).[27] The percentage of white twenty-five- to twenty-nine-year-olds attaining bachelor's degrees climbed from 29 percent to 43 percent over the twenty-year period following 1995. The increase for blacks was much less—from 15 percent to 21 percent.[28]

The civil rights revolution reduced prejudice and discrimination for many in the upper echelon of society, but the expansion of the welfare state and the introduction of a wide array of affirmative action policies did not translate into anything close to social or economic equality for a broad spectrum of the black population. Instead of resolving Myrdal's dilemma, they may have had a perverse effect. As black journalist Jason Riley observes, "The intentions behind welfare programs may be noble. But in practice they have slowed the self-development that proved necessary for other groups to advance."[29]

The End of American Exceptionalism?

Slavery's legacy is not the only concern troubling Americans in the twenty-first century's second decade. A number of the pillars of American exceptionalism seem to be crumbling. The frontier is long gone. Worker wages have stagnated as productivity growth has slowed from 3 percent to 1 percent. The country's schools, which were once the world's leaders, are now producing students who cannot keep pace with their peers abroad.[30] Integrating immigrants into the mainstream of American society becomes more complicated when over 25 percent of the country's 40 million foreign-born residents are unauthorized.[31] Those who control the culture-defining institutions of the society— universities, museums, public entertainment, and national news outlets, the new nobility, it might be said—are defining a strict set of beliefs with respect to climate change, affirmative action, and the legitimacy of inequalities that they expect the rest of society to accept. When religions are established, the people's liberties are placed at risk.

Citizen participation is high, but its impact has been warped by the vast expansion of political primaries as the method for selecting presidents, governors, senators, and members of the House of Representatives in the aftermath of the violence surrounding the Democratic convention of 1968. Many of these primary contests are low-visibility elections that attract as little as 5 percent to 10 percent of the eligible electorate. Candidates must take positions designed to please the most engaged and extreme partisans. Room for moderation and compromise across party lines has been sharply reduced.

Meanwhile, the US welfare state has expanded so rapidly that it is beginning to resemble those of many European countries. The number of adults receiving disability benefits has doubled from four million in 1995 to just shy of nine million in 2016. Nearly 14 percent of all households were receiving food stamps in 2013, a doubling of the percentage since 2001. Medicaid enrollment also doubled in the twenty-first century, increasing from 34.5 million in 2000 to 54.5 million in 2010 and, with the enactment of the Affordable Care Act in that year, escalating to 70.5 million in 2016.[32] The steep growth in these entitlement programs, combined with the rapid growth in Social Security and Medicare costs driven by an aging population, is placing extreme pressure on the national fiscal. The federal debt as a percentage of GDP has more than doubled over the course of the twenty-first century—from about 36 percent in 2000 to roughly 78 percent in 2017, with future growth projected to around 90 percent by 2027.[33]

Most seriously, political power has become increasingly centralized. The executive branch is discovering new tools by which it can take action without securing the cooperation of the legislature. The desire to halt climate change by containing carbon dioxide emissions has unleashed a set of regulatory controls over major parts of the economy. Power continues to shift away from state and local levels of government to the national government. Most if not all of these developments are driven by committed, public-spirited reformers, the very thing that Tocqueville feared.

Was Tocqueville correct when he said democracies could not endure? When he identified America as exceptional, did he just get the timeline wrong? Americans have enjoyed their freedoms for their first 225 years, but how much longer will the practical, individualistic, "earthward" elements in American political culture endure? Has America been exceptional only in that the urge to reform, to centralize power, to undermine individual autonomy has taken longer to reach full fruition? Or does the idea of a free society still endure? These questions are currently under strenuous debate. The outcome is unclear. No one can say with any certainty whether the changes taking place during the first years of the twenty-first century will be reversed or accelerated during the remaining ones. Our best hope is, as Benjamin Franklin said, that America is still "a republic if we can keep it."

Notes

1. Jonah Goldberg, "Liberals Believe in Holding America Back," *National Review,* November 10, 2010. Obama made the observation in 2008. In 2016 he seemed to alter that position when he said at the Democratic National Convention, "These values my grandparents taught me—they haven't gone anywhere. They're as strong as ever; still cherished by people of every party, every race, and every faith. They live on in each of us. . . . What makes us American, what makes us patriots, is what's in here [at this convention hall]. That's what matters. That's why we can take the food and music and holidays and styles of other countries, and blend it into something uniquely our own." Ron Fournier, "Obama's New American Exceptionalism," *Atlantic,* July 28, 2016. Still, he said the United States was unique, not that it was exceptional.

2. Vladimir V. Putin, "A Plea for Caution from Russia," *New York Times,* September 11, 2013.

3. Abraham Lincoln, quoted in Eric Bjornlund, *Beyond Free and Fair: Monitoring Elections and Building Democracy* (Washington, DC: Woodrow Wilson Center Press), 20.

4. Abraham Lincoln, *Second Annual Message,* December 1, 1862.

5. Abraham Lincoln, *Gettysberg Address,* November 19, 1863.

6. Proof that Lincoln read Tocqueville is lacking, but these ideas were very much a part of the thinking of Henry Clay, Lincoln's political lodestar.

7. Alexis de Tocqueville, *Democracy in America,* ed. Eduardo Nolla, trans. James T. Schleifer, vol. 2 (Indianapolis: Liberty Fund, 2012).

8. Tocqueville, *Democracy in America,* vol. 2, part 1, 768–69.

9. Ralph Bunche, quoted in Gunnar Myrdal, *An American Dilemma: The Negro Problem and Modern Democracy,* vol. 1, 6th ed. (New Brunswick, NJ: Transaction Publishers, 2009), 4.

10. Louis Hartz, *The Liberal Tradition in America* (1955; repr., New York: Harvest, 1991).

11. Reinhard Bendix argues that the working class was mobilized for radical political action in Europe because it was simultaneously deprived of a legitimate status in both the political and economic spheres of the society. Reinhard Bendix, *Nation-Building and Citizenship: Studies of Our Changing Social Order* (Berkeley, University of California Press, Ltd., 1964). Also see Seymour M. Lipset and Gary W. Marks, *It Didn't Happen Here: Why Socialism Failed in America* (New York: W. W. Norton, 2001).

12. Alberto Alesina, Rafael Di Tella, and Robert MacCulloch, "Inequality and Happiness: Are Europeans and Americans Different?" *Journal of Public Economics* 88 (2004): 2011.

13. Morris Fiorina, Paul E. Peterson, Bertram Johnson, and William G. Mayer, *The New American Democracy,* 7th ed. (New York: Pearson, 2011), 111.

14. Fiorina et al., *New American Democracy,* 111.

15. Alberto Alesina, Stefanie Stantcheva, and Edoardo Teso, "Intergenerational Mobility and Preferences for Redistribution," *National Bureau of Economic Research,* Working Paper 23027, January 2017, tables 5, 9.

16. Alesina, Di Tella, and MacCulloch, "Inequality and Happiness," 2011.

17. "The wages of labour . . . are much higher in North America than in any part of England. But though North America is not so rich as England, it is much more thriving, and advancing with much greater rapidity to the further acquisition of riches." Adam Smith, *The Wealth of Nations,* Cannon ed. (1776; repr., London: Methuen, 1930), 71–72, quoted in Milton Friedman and Anna J. Schwartz, *Monetary Trends in the United States and the United Kingdom: Their Relation to Income, Prices, and Interest Rates, 1865–1975* (Chicago: University of Chicago Press, 1982), 139.

18. Frederick Jackson Turner, "The Significance of the Frontier in American History," paper read at the meeting of the American Historical Association, Chicago, July 12, 1893.

19. Alexis de Tocqueville, *Journey to America,* ed. J. P. Mayer, trans. George Lawrence (Westport, Conn.: Greenwood Press, 1959), 283.

20. Alexis de Tocqueville, *Democracy in America,* ed. Eduardo Nolla, trans. James T. Schleifer, vol. 2, part 2 (Indianapolis: Liberty Fund, 2012), 896.

21. Claudia Goldin, "The Human Capital Century: Has U.S. Leadership Come to an End?" *Education Next* 3, no. 1 (Winter 2003).

22. Max Roser and Mohamad Nagdy, "Primary Education," 2016, https://ourworldindata.org/primary-education-and-schools (accessed April 12, 2017).

23. Fiorina et al., *New American Democracy,* 119.

24. Jacob Vigdor, "The Civic and Cultural Assimilation of Immigrants to the United States," in *The Economics of Immigration: Market-Based Approaches, Social Science, and Public Policy,* ed. Benjamin Powell (New York: Oxford University Press, 2015), 89-90.

25. Gunnar Myrdal, *The American Dilemma: The Negro Problem and American Society* (New York: Harper, 1944), ch. 1, pp. 3-4.

26. Henry Kaiser Foundation, "Poverty Rate by Race/Ethnicity, 2015," http://kff.org/other/state-indicator/poverty-rate-by-raceethnicity/?currentTimeframe (accessed April 12, 2017).

27. Christopher Jencks and Sara McLanahan, "Was Moynihan Right? What Happens to Children of Unmarried Mothers," *Education Next* 15, no. 2 (Spring 2015), figure 1.

28. Mikhail Zinshteyn, "College Graduation Rates Rise, but Racial Gaps Persist and Men Still Out-earn Women," *Hechinger Report,* May 26, 2016.

29 Jason L. Riley, *Please Stop Helping Us: How Liberals Make It Harder for Blacks to Succeed* (New York: Encounter Books, 2014), 3.

30. Among American children with at least one parent who went to college, the percentage proficient in mathematics is 43 percent, as compared to 73 percent in Korea and 71 percent in Poland. Eric A. Hanushek, Paul E. Peterson, and Ludger Woessmann, *Endangering Prosperity: A Global View of the American School* (Washington, DC: Brookings, 2013), 40.

31. Jens Mauel Krogstad, Jeffrey S. Passel, and D'Vera Cohn, "Five Facts about Illegal Immigration in the U.S.," *Fact Tank—Our Lives in Numbers*, November 2, 2016; Fred Dews, "What Percentage of U.S. Population Is Foreign Born?" *Brookings Now*, October 3, 2013, https://www.brookings.edu/blog/brookings-now/2013/10/03/what-percentage-of-u-s-population-is-foreign-born (accessed March 22, 2017).

32. *Statista*, "Total Medicaid Enrollment from 1966 to 2016," https://www.statista.com/statistics/245347/total-medicaid-enrollment-since-1966 (accessed March 22, 2017).

33. Congressional Budget Office, "The Budget and Economic Outlook: 2017–2027," https://www.cbo.gov/sites/default/files/115th-congress-2017-2018/reports/52370-budeconoutlook.pdf (accessed March 22, 2017). For total public debt, see Federal Reserve Bank of St. Louis and U.S. Office of Management and Budget, Economic Research: Federal Debt: Total Public Debt as Percent of Gross Domestic Product [GFDEGDQ188S], https://fred.stlouisfed.org/series/GFDEGDQ188S (accessed March 22, 2017).

2

Legal Origins of American Exceptionalism

MICHAEL McCONNELL

On a cold February day, uniformed officers in the city of Boston, Massachusetts, shot and killed five unarmed young men. Naturally, the community was in an uproar. There were massive public protests. Some political leaders and agitators exploited these killings, labeling them a "massacre" before there had even been time for a public inquiry. There were insistent demands for systemic change. Agitators distributed selective accounts of the event, featuring altered images presenting the officers in the worst possible light. No matter what the actual facts may have been, the officers were portrayed as oppressors. Protesters insisted they should be prosecuted, convicted, and punished.

The eight officers involved in the shootings were indeed prosecuted. They might well have been convicted and punished to mollify the angry public, if not for the commitment of one young lawyer to the rule of law. His name was John Adams. Naturally, Adams assumed that defending the perpetrators of the Boston Massacre would be the end of his political career, but defend them he did.

Adams summoned witnesses before the jury to develop the facts of what really had happened. Facts matter, not just appearances or mere emotional responses to events. Then, in a summation that is still one of the great documents of the law in the United States, Adams quoted to the jury the law pertaining to the case. He told them that, if the British soldiers had "reason to believe that they were in danger of attack," the shooting would be "justifiable or, at least, excusable." That is, the soldiers didn't actually need to have been in danger for the shooting to be justified. Rather, to reach a not-guilty verdict on the basis of self-defense, the jury had only to be convinced that the soldiers had fired in the *belief* that they were in danger.

More important, Adams spoke to the jury about the importance of following the law even at a time of great emotion. He told them that we were engaged in the struggle for liberty and property, but if we "cut up the law" (his words), the rest would be of little value. "Rules of law," he said, "should be universally known whatever effect they may have on politics." Even more remarkable than the fact that John Adams stepped up to this task of legal representation was that the jury agreed with him. Six of the eight defendants were acquitted outright, and two of them, the ones who were most directly responsible for firing into the crowd, were convicted on reduced charges and given a relatively mild punishment: they were branded on the thumb.

The city of Boston did not descend into riots in response to this verdict. Quite the contrary: the Boston Massacre and the acquittal of the soldiers became a point of pride and one of the hallmarks of the American Revolution. For John Adams had made a point that resonated with his countrymen: a revolution to vindicate the legal rights of American colonists must uphold the legal rights of all.

As Adams said—and as the jury thought, too—fidelity to law is essential, whatever effect it may have on politics. Historians tell us that the American Revolution was remarkably law abiding for a rebellion, especially in contrast to the democratic revolution that was going on at roughly the same time across the Atlantic, in the streets of Paris. In Paris, if anyone like John Adams was speaking up for law, nobody was listening to him. Instead, there were guillotines, confiscations of property, political trials, mob vengeance, and lots of blood.

The American Revolution was so very different. The Tea Partiers, when they were attacking those vessels in Boston Harbor, scrupulously refrained from taking any private property—any cargo other than the tea that was their political symbol. In fact, when one small item belonging to a captain was broken, the protesters paid to replace it. When one participant in the Tea Party slipped into his pocket some of the tea the others were throwing into the harbor, he was apprehended and severely punished.

This respect for law and for property was intentional and deeply self-conscious. Listen to the words of Thomas Paine in *Common Sense,* the most widely read pamphlet of the American Revolution. "Where, says some, is the king of America? I tell you, friend, that in America the law is king. For as in absolute governments the king is law, so in free countries the law ought to be king and there ought to be no other."

What is the rule of law? The answer rests on two propositions. The first is that we govern ourselves through known, settled, understandable rules that apply to everyone. The second is that these rules are applied equally and dispassionately, through fair processes and procedures. The rule of law is not a libertarian notion. We can have small government, or we can have big government. Lawfulness is a question of *how* government operates. This rule of law produces a just and prosperous society. In a society observing the rule of law, people have the ability to plan and to invest for the future. Law, just as much as economics and maybe even more so, is the bedrock of prosperity and thus the bedrock of American exceptionalism.

Some worry about declining American exceptionalism, and there may have been some decline in the strength of the rule of law as well. But that does not mean we should despair of our commitment to law. I believe that, for the most part, American life is still governed by laws applied reasonably dispassionately and through reasonably fair processes. Yet we certainly should not take this for granted. There are problems.

What are the threats today to the rule of law? There are plenty, but I want to mention four and concentrate especially on one. The first is politicized law enforcement. There are dangerous indications that federal and state regulatory agencies have become tools of partisan politics to a degree not seen before. The most conspicuous instance is the targeting by Internal Revenue Service personnel of organizations that were the political opponents of the administration. Even based on what is publicly known, this is the most extreme example of political abuse of power since Richard Nixon. As expressed by the United States Court of Appeals for the Sixth Circuit, "Among the most serious allegations a federal court can address are that an executive agency has targeted citizens for mistreatment based on their political views. No citizen, Republican or Democrat, Socialist or Libertarian, should be targeted or even have to fear being targeted on these grounds." Perhaps more frightening than the behavior of the IRS, however, was the relative indifference of much of the press and political Washington to that abuse. In August 2016, an opinion by the Court of Appeals for the DC Circuit found that those practices have not yet ceased, that they are still continuing. That should have been front-page news.

We have seen similarly blatant partisan abuse of the justice system at the state level. In Wisconsin from May 2010 to May 2012, prosecutors and police raided private homes in the dark of night and seized private computers and files of conservative political organizations, leaking one-sided accounts of the investigation to the press—all in pursuit of what courts eventually concluded was an entirely baseless investigation of constitutionally protected activity. In Texas, partisan prosecutors brought charges against Governor Rick Perry for the crime of threatening to veto legislation that he disagreed with. That's not a crime. The case was eventually dismissed. But the cost in time, resources, and public reputation is fearsome. The harm to our political system has been done.

I worked for the Department of Justice for a number of years and have a great deal of faith in the professionalism of that department and of the FBI, but in the wake of seemingly disparate treatment of such political figures as Scooter Libby, Governor Bob McDonnell, Jon Corzine, David Petraeus, and, dare I say it, Hillary Clinton, many are now wondering whether the Department of Justice and the FBI also have been compromised.

Politicized law *enforcement* is a threat to American democracy, but we are also seeing more politicized law *interpretation*. This is where the courts decide cases, especially about hot-button constitutional questions, in light of their own political predilections and the movements to which they belong, rather than according to what the Constitution and the laws say. This, in turn, has engendered increasing politicization of the process by which federal judges are nominated and confirmed. And this has now been going on, certainly, since the unfortunate events surrounding the confirmation to the Supreme Court of Judge Robert Bork.

Every presidential administration has gotten more extreme in this regard. Each one is worse than the one before, and I think that this is taking a toll. I still believe that the US federal judiciary is one of the great judiciaries of the world, but we cannot be complacent about that in light of this tendency to use the power vested in the courts to accomplish what are essentially political rather than legal ends.

Another problem is a disregard for constitutional limits, particularly in the executive branch. Since the time of George Washington, we have depended very heavily upon the idea that the executive branch and its officials and lawyers will comply with the law. Not because someone's going to punish them if they don't, but because it is the solemn duty of a government official or a government lawyer to follow the law. But self-restraint has been weakening. One astonishing example is that the prior administration spent some $7 billion from the federal Treasury that had not been appropriated by Congress. Both the Government Accountability Office and the federal district court concluded that these expenditures had been in violation of the law. That, too, should have been front-page news.

The last threat to the rule of law, and the one that I want to comment on in the most detail, has to do with transformations in the administrative state. There has been a significant shift, even in the time since I began teaching law in the mid-1980s, in the way in which executive agencies operate. What I worry about here is a combination of vast, perplexing, and incomprehensible laws passed by Congress, coupled with very broad administrative discretion as to individual cases. The result is an erosion of any idea that these cases are really governed by rules. Rather, they succumb to case-by-case arbitrariness, with baneful effects on democratic accountability, equality, and prosperity.

One example from the financial regulatory sector is the original banking act of 1864, the first one of its kind in the United States. It was twenty-nine pages long. Similarly, the Federal Reserve Act of 1913, one of the most important acts in American history with regard to the financial sector, was thirty-two pages long. The Dodd-Frank bill came in at over 1,600 pages. This was not the bill of which the then Speaker of the House said, "We have to pass the bill so that you can find out what is in it," but it might as well have been. Very few people know what's in it, and it's almost impossible to read. The *Economist* magazine called it "virtually incomprehensible from any perspective." It contains a rule called the Volcker Rule that was originally expressed by former Federal Reserve chairman Paul Volcker in a single sentence: "The banks insured by the government may not engage in proprietary trading." It took the Dodd-Frank bill eleven pages to incorporate that one sentence into law. And the proposed regulations defining that one sentence come in at 298 pages.

Increased length, complexity, and incomprehensibility in law may provide employment for a lot of lawyers, but it defeats the rule of law, and the Founders knew this. They tried to warn against it. James Madison wrote, in Federalist essay number 62, that it would be "of little avail to the people that the laws are made by men of their own choice if the laws be so voluminous that they cannot be read or so incoherent that they cannot be understood."

The second feature that worries me here is a shift to case-by-case determinations. When I studied administrative law, under Professor Antonin Scalia of blessed memory, I assumed that the way in which agencies operate most of the time—because this is what the Administrative Procedure Act is all about—is by regulation and adjudications, which is to say, regulations are rules and adjudications are applications of those rules.

This is a reflection of the very ideal of the rule of law: we have rules, and we apply them dispassionately. The modern trend in administrative procedure, however, is to operate instead through case-by-case decision making of two forms. First, there are licenses. That's where the regulated party has to go to the agency and ask permission to act. I call this "Mother, may I?" regulation. Instead of a rule telling you what you have to do, you go to Washington and you tell them what you want to do, and they say yes or no: "Mother, may I?"

Second, there are waivers, which grant permission to do something different from whatever the rules require. Officials enforcing the Affordable Care Act, in the first couple of years, gave 1,231 waivers from its requirements. Four hundred and fifty of those went to labor unions. Most of the others went to large corporations, including Pepsi and McDonald's. Other applicants that asked for waivers were denied. We have no idea why some are granted and some are denied. This is not, I submit to you, the rule of law. This is the rule of men.

One of the great Supreme Court justices, Robert Jackson, a Franklin Delano Roosevelt appointee, said, "There is no more effective practical guarantee against arbitrary and unreasonable government than to require that the principles of law which officials would impose upon a minority must be imposed generally. Conversely, nothing opens the door to arbitrary action so effectively as to allow those officials to pick and choose only a few to whom they will apply legislation, and, thus, to escape the political retribution that might be visited upon them if larger numbers were affected."

When we have a law that requires 1,231 exceptions in particular cases, given to politically powerful entities, it is an indication that something is awry. It means either that the general rule was very badly concocted to begin with (otherwise why would we need that many exceptions?) or that special favors are being traded. It might mean both.

Who benefits from this kind of a system? That's always a question. Things are not done randomly. Things in Washington don't just happen. Who benefits? James Madison gave us the answer, over two hundred years ago: complicated and incomprehensible laws give an "unreasonable advantage . . . to the sagacious, the enterprising, and the moneyed few, over the industrious and uninformed mass of the people."

This complex, case-by-case regulatory system certainly benefits lobbyists and lawyers. According to the *Economist,* the leading financial industry trade association employed 5,490 people to work with the various subcommittees of Congress in connection with Dodd-Frank. They are awake, the rest of us are asleep. They know what's going on, but nobody else has a clue.

Large firms also benefit. Even when regulation imposes costs on the large firms, they still benefit relative to their smaller competitors because they are large enough to have regulatory lawyers and offices and so forth. Smaller firms don't. The next time you see the CEO of a large corporation being patted on the back for his public spiritedness in agreeing to regulation of one sort or another—whether minimum wage or labor regulation or environmental greenness—check your wallets. They are not being beneficent, nor should they. I'm not criticizing. Large firms gain an advantage in the competitive world by having regulations that impose relatively greater costs on smaller competitors than on them.

I have a friend who, with his brother, co-owns a business worth a few million dollars in sales, a small business in the great scheme of things. My friend likes to support libertarian candidates for office. He told me his brother pleads with him to stop making those contributions because they have so many contacts with regulators, many in California at the state level, not all federal. Those regulators have discretion to either get in their face or not—so much discretion. His brother is convinced that those people that they're meeting with check opensecrets.com, find out where the contributions are going, and treat regulated businesses accordingly. I have no idea if that's right, but I will say there's motive and opportunity.

The rule of law is at the heart of American self-identity, as Thomas Paine said. The rule of law is still, I think, very strong, especially when we compare ourselves to other places around the world. But there are worrying trends to which we should be alert. What can be done about them? This is not an easy question, to say the least. The traditions and institutions behind the rule of law take decades to develop, but they can be destroyed, if not in an instant, then at least in an administration. To reverse this, we need a different approach to both legislation and regulation, one emphasizing clarity, employing simpler rules, reducing case-by-case discretion, and bringing about greater transparency.

To do this, we need various dimensions of reform. Intellectual reform is where I would begin. There's a lot of thought to be done about how to construct our regulatory state in a way that has more fidelity to the rule of law. The 1947 Administrative Procedure Act is way out of date and barely even describes the way the federal government now operates. A Hoover Institution task force I am heading with Charles Calomiris has been working with scholars in law, economics, political science, and history to develop ideas about how the administrative state might be reformed and brought back in accord with the rule of law.

In addition to thinking, we need a new commitment to the common good and greater understanding of economics. We need legislative reform. Congress is no longer operating, really. It's a very strange institution. Just the fact that the two houses are run by Republicans doesn't mean it's actually doing a very good job.

But on some level I'm hopeful about the distrust in government, because I believe we need a new skepticism about the wisdom, modus operandi, and capacity of bureaucratic agencies. We should not assume that they are just dispassionate experts promoting the public good.

Ordinary Americans are asking the question, what is going wrong? I think the first answer is that the rule of law is beginning to erode. That is why it is so urgent to recognize the connection between American exceptionalism and rule of law. If we could hew to the law in the maelstrom of the Boston Massacre, we should be able to do so today.

3

American Exceptionalism

Due Principally to Secure
Private Property Rights

GARY LIBECAP

The United States has been unusual in its protection of property, especially in the realm of physical resources like land but also with regard to intellectual property and encouraging innovation.

This is not surprising given that most early immigrants, at least, came from places where individuals had few rights to land or other resources: these were all held by the state through the king or other authority, and so those rights came to be enshrined in the US Constitution with protections against the taking of property without just compensation. In terms of threats to property rights and American exceptionalism, this "takings" issue is distinctive, not least in terms of natural resources.

Take environmental regulation. Don't get me wrong: I do like the environment, and I am concerned about the environment, but the environment can become a very convenient tool to undermine property rights and all of the benefits that they provide. We have this protection in the Bill of Rights and also in the delegation of powers clause. The idea is to restrict the power of the state vis-à-vis individual assent in a private society and a market economy.

Why are private property rights so critical? For one thing, they assign authority over resources to individuals, not the state. It is individuals who make decisions about production, investment, and reallocation. Markets and individuals become the primary drivers of economic activity, reallocation, and decisions about resource use. This is absolutely essential for a free society. If the state were the primary decision maker, or the property right were very subservient to the state, then we would live in a very different society and a very different kind of economy.

The longer the time period during which the property right naturally exists, the more durable the decision making can be. In the longer term, people can consider decisions about investment and other economic activities. The more secure the property right, the more risk people will be willing to take in their investment and economic activities. Uncertainty with regard to the property right regime only exacerbates the other natural uncertainties that may exist through market or other external conditions. The more secure and longer term the right is, the greater the ability to trade and the higher the expected returns from private economic activity are. This is what leads to a dynamic, growing economy and encourages long-term economic growth. This pattern is attributable to an American exceptionalism based on the historical security of property rights.

What are the threats to all of this good news? A primary one is environmental regulation—an expansive regulatory overreach, or broadening interpretation of important environmental laws, to restrict private decision making. The Clean Air Act; the Clean Water Act; the Endangered Species Act; NEPA (the National Environmental Policy Act)—these are the four pillars, and every state has its comparable environmental legislation. So long as these laws adhere to the original intent in drafting them—under which private property rights are protected—there is little to be concerned about in terms of requiring cleaner air or water. But when agencies broaden their interpretation of the law, they become part of the problem.

Where does this occur, for example, in the Clean Water Act, and why is this so difficult for a landowner? One area is in the definition of a navigable stream. Initially, federal law was restricted to navigable waterways, but over time that definition has been stretched so that almost any waterway can be defined or designated as navigable. That means that the federal agencies, under the Clean Water Act, actually might claim authority over them. It is very costly for a landowner to challenge an agency if it makes a ruling to restrict activity in agricultural or urban development, or manufacturing, or any matter, because it is within agencies, and within the administrative process, that rulings are reconsidered. The decks are stacked against landowners, and it becomes prohibitively expensive to challenge rulings.

We also see this overreach in the Clean Air Act, in defining what is a pollutant and what activities constitute significant contributions to air pollution. But perhaps the most egregious is the Endangered Species Act. Nobody wants to see a species become extinct, but there has to be some sort of rational balance. Unfortunately, the Endangered Species Act specifically prohibits cost-benefit analysis. Essentially, the species are assigned infinite value, and costs associated with their protection are not regarded. We have about 1,600 species listed, and only thirty-three out of those have been successfully de-listed. It's very politicized to put a species on a list, and equally politicized to take it off, because all sorts of groups benefit from these measures. The act puts many restrictions on land use in order to protect habitat. This can be counterproductive to protecting a species because landowners know this, so it sometimes is in their interest, frankly, to destroy the creatures. And should they observe this potentially endangered species threatening their own interests, they may be motivated to destroy it before somebody else finds out that it's there, which certainly runs counter to the objective and spirit of the law.

In this and other matters, what is gradually happening, as compared to the early period of American history, is that the state is becoming increasingly important in terms of monitoring and determining which areas of private decision making are acceptable, a trend that is weakening property rights. This comes from a broader definition of the public's role, or of the public good, in deciding whether private decisions are commensurate with public interest. That is the open door for regulatory "mission creep."

Over time, the American position with regard to the security of property rights has declined. In the early part of this century, the United States was always ranked first; but recently, in some indexes, we're down to forty-first. Today, there are other places, such as Finland and New Zealand, that provide more definite property rights.

Fracking provides an illustration of the problem. It's a very emotional issue where I teach, at the University of California–Santa Barbara, but it sheds light on the role of secure property rights and innovation and on how regulatory restrictions can inhibit beneficial activities.

Fracking is the hydraulic fracturing of subsurface material followed by directional drilling, which allows for a single well to reach a wide area in order to access hydrocarbons. The process propelled the United States from a country that was thought to have been at peak supply—which was going to be a national security problem—to one that is in a far more secure position in terms of the energy it needs to drive prosperity. Fracking reduced greenhouse gas emissions by allowing for cheaper natural gas. In energy production, the lower costs owed to fracking have encouraged the relocation and reinvigoration of manufacturing. Indeed, it has been beneficial on almost every level, not least by adding about $1,200 in disposable income to the average American pocket and accounting for much of the reduction in carbon dioxide emissions in the United States.

This innovation was exclusively a US activity: the exploration and innovation applied, in new ways, techniques that had been around for a while. Why did that happen in the United States and not elsewhere?

It's not because we have the largest reserves but because we have had the most beneficial property rights regime.

Americans, for the most part, own their mineral rights. But if you're a surface landowner in some other nation, the state owns them. That is the standard situation in most countries. And if the government undertook or considered fracking or some similar activity on your land, you would bear all the costs, and the benefits would be broadly spread. You would have very little incentive to agree to that. In the United States that's not likely to happen. You have mineral rights to oil and gas below your surface property, and you can share it and any of the benefits. This provides incentives for individual landowners to be part of a wider energy progress.

Notably, most fracking in the United States takes place on private, not federal, lands, where the federal government has to decide where this will take place for most of the recoverable reserve slot. This is a good empirical test of the importance of property rights relative to natural endowments. In many countries, especially in Europe, fracking has been so politicized that it's been banned.

Today, the United States is where the action is in terms of fracking: 95 percent of all wells involved in fracking are drilled in the United States, even though most of the reserves lie on federal lands. It's the property rights regime that explains this. It's very hard to get the Bureau of Land Management, for example, to approve any new wells, and the Obama administration added numerous restrictions on fracking on federal lands.

Fracking is a concrete example of an activity that involved American ingenuity and American innovation. It's had positive benefits, and yet it takes place almost solely where private property rights are secure—that is, where American exceptionalism has been in force.

4

Intellectual Property as a Pillar of American Exceptionalism

STEPHEN HABER

Usually we associate property rights with physical property. I have a property right to a bottle of water until I drink it all. I have a property right to my house and to my car. But most of the important property rights in the modern economy are intangible property rights. If we think about the market caps of the big corporations in the United States today, many of them don't really have much in the way of physical assets. What are the physical assets of Facebook? It's a bunch of kids with hoodies. The hoodies probably have some value in the secondary market but not much. The value is in the intellectual property of the firm.

Permit me an example of how intellectual property is also key in a more traditional industry: oil and gas. What does intellectual property have to do with the fracking revolution? Almost all of the innovations that enabled the first horizontal drilling, and then the combinations of water, chemicals, and sand to keep the fractured rocks open, were patented. One of the reasons why Midland Texas is among the wealthiest communities in the United States, with a per capita income higher than that of Silicon Valley, is the US property rights system. If you had taken away all those intellectual property rights that encouraged people to develop the technology for fracking, there would have been no fracking.

The value of intellectual property was recognized by the writers of the US Constitution. In fact, the only specific property right they wrote into the Constitution was the one pertaining to patents and copyrights. Article 1, section 8 reads: Congress shall have the power "to promote the progress of science and useful Arts, by securing for limited Times to Authors and Inventors the exclusive Right to their respective Writings and Discoveries."

One of the first things the first Congress did was to pass the Patent Act of 1790. This was a really unusual thing for a government to have done. Most countries, up to that point, did not have patent systems. Great Britain had one, but it was extremely cumbersome and costly. Although there were some important patents taken out in eighteenth-century England—and the evidence indicates that they helped promote the Industrial Revolution—patenting was not something that was broadly undertaken by the population.

The United States went in a very unusual direction for the time. The idea was that patents were going to be an administrative procedure of the government. That is, the government would not decide whether a patent was valid or not. That would be left to the courts. Americans would register their patents, paying a very small fee—about five dollars, or roughly 5 percent of the price of getting a patent in Great Britain. There was no special act of Parliament required, no need to obtain any special favor, and thus no need to pay any bribes.

The patentee, unlike under British law, had to be the first and true inventor anywhere in the world. That meant that the patent wasn't given to whoever got to the patent office first but rather to the person who actually invented the technology or idea first. The invention then had to be available to the public immediately. That is, the patent had to be specified, when it was issued, so that when the patent term ran out it could be copied.

The purpose of this was to democratize invention and encourage innovation. It was not to create a bunch of monopolies. The whole point of a patent is that it confers property rights that can be licensed to somebody else. If anyone actually invents something that could not be backward engineered, they would never patent it; rather, they would keep it a trade secret and have a monopoly, like Coca-Cola, for which there is no patent, or Thomas' English Muffins, for which there is no patent. These are closely held trade secrets.

The point of the US patent system wasn't to create monopolies. That's not what the Founders wanted to do. They wanted to give people incentives to transact with each other, and when you create a property right, you create an incentive to trade or license that right. The whole system was based on the notion that there would be people who were inventors, and there would be people who would implement those inventions, and there would be people in between who specialize in writing contracts between inventors and implementers. Abraham Lincoln, in fact, was one of them. He was a patent attorney in the nineteenth century.

From the point of view of the inventor, the patent gave him or her—there were a lot of women inventors even in the nineteenth century—the ability to appropriate their returns from the investment they had made in developing a technology. From the point of view of society, the patent is a property right that serves as the basis for any number of contracts that can be written among all the interested parties. If you took away the property right, the whole system of contracting would break down.

Permit me an example. How many patents are there connected to a smartphone? Nobody's sure, but it's in excess of ten thousand. It may be in the hundreds of thousands. There is a complex of legal reasons why nobody knows. There are dozens of companies that own all the different patents that make a smartphone work. If you took away the patents, it would be impossible for firms to contract with each other to put a supercomputer in your pocket that will geolocate, record video, send data around the globe to anybody, do any kind of calculation you want, and also happen to be useful for making a phone call. What makes that thing work is all the patents in it, and it's a remarkable testament to the ability of property rights to create a web of contracts to produce a product that is valued around the globe, so much so that there are now more cell phones than there are adult human beings on the planet. The average global selling price for a smartphone is $300—which is why kids in the United States treat them as toys.

The purpose of patents was not to create monopolies, but many of the attacks on patents take the position that patents are a government-created monopoly. That is a fundamentally incorrect way to think about a patent: it is a property right. It's no more a government-created monopoly than the property right to your house is a government-created monopoly on your home.

The response to the 1790 Patent Act was remarkable. Thomas Jefferson, who was the first head of the patent office, was initially skeptical about patents. He changed his mind very quickly. There were hundreds of patents taken out within the first decade of the passage of the act. They were predominantly manufacturing patents, often being taken out by quite common people.

Among America's most notable nineteenth-century patentees was Abraham Lincoln, who patented, in 1849, a device that would raise and lower boats going up and down the Ohio River. We now think of the Ohio as navigable. But there were sandbars in the Ohio until the Army Corps of Engineers removed them. Lincoln's invention essentially put canvas bags on the side of a boat with a bellows that could be used to blow up the bags with air, lift the boat, and take it over the shoals. Lincoln himself, of course, was neither a boatman nor a manufacturer—he was a lawyer—but the idea was that he would license this patent. Nobody ever took it up—a fact that is hardly surprising because most patents never get commercialized.

Why the focus on intellectual property among the Founders? We're very fortunate to live in an amazingly prosperous society, but this was not the case for Americans in 1790. Think back to the American Revolution. Had Great Britain not been at war with France, we would still be calling English muffins "crumpets." The Revolutionary War was won because Americans could count on French soldiers, French mercenaries, the French navy, and French money. The reason France was crucial was because the thirteen colonies were poor and Great Britain was rich.

Circa 1700, the American colonies had a GDP about equal to that of Brazil at the time. Circa 1790, we were not only poor, we were deeply in debt. The Founding Fathers wish they had our debt problems today. The debt-to-GDP ratio was somewhere in the area of four or five to one. The country was broke, in a depression, and the Founders were quite concerned that if we didn't do something to create a robust economy, we were going to become a colony of somebody else. So they embraced the concept of property rights—particularly intellectual property rights—as a spur to innovation and economic growth.

What was the result of the property rights approach of which intellectual property rights are a very strong part? The US economy took off. By 1820, we were about one-quarter to one-third as rich as Great Britain or Germany. By 1850, we were starting to approach parity with Germany and were closing in on Great Britain. By 1870, we passed Germany and reached parity with Great Britain. By 1890, we were ahead of everybody. By 1910, shortly before World War I, we already had a GDP about twice that of Germany or Great Britain. By 1930, we hit about three times that. By 1940, our GDP was approaching three and a half times those of Germany and Great Britain.

Why did the United States win World War II? We didn't have better generals. We had brave soldiers, but our enemies had brave soldiers, too. We simply outproduced the Axis powers. Why were we able to do that?

Because we had a property rights system, of which intellectual property rights were a key part, that incentivized invention and innovation. If there is a central lesson in American history for the rest of the world, it's that if you want to be wealthy, you need property rights.

Last year, I was lecturing about this in China. I kept talking about property rights, and they looked at me as if to say, "Of course we have property rights." It finally dawned on me, that whenever I was saying property rights, they were thinking, "Well, the state owns everything." They have property rights, but they are collective property rights. Private property rights took several hours to explain. I thought it was just my New York accent.

In the United States, the Silicon Valley of the late nineteenth century was Cleveland. The electrical machinery industry was a Cleveland industry, made up of lots of small and medium-size firms. There were some big giants eventually, such as Westinghouse and General Electric, but what's so interesting about the electrical machinery industry is how many small firms there were operating in it, all filing patents, all defending their property rights. And the courts were protecting those rights. In short, the patent system allowed the American electrical machinery industry to leapfrog over its major competitor, Germany.

What do we know from economic historians and the work of development economists? There are no wealthy countries without strong patents. As property rights become stronger, and intellectual property rights become stronger, GDP increases. Causality runs from the property rights to GDP, not from GDP to the property rights.

This brings us to a puzzle. Why is it that courts, legislatures, and recent presidents have tried to weaken patent rights? If there's a theme about property rights in the past eight years or so, it's that intellectual property rights are bad and are blocking innovation. In 2006, the Supreme Court, in the eBay decision, made it harder to obtain an injunction, that is, a stay order, against an infringer. It used to be that if people were infringing your patent, you could get an injunction to stop them from producing and selling. It's now very hard to get an injunction, which has discouraged innovation.

The America Invents Act of 2011 removed the "first to invent" feature of our system and replaced it with a "first to file" feature. It also created an administrative court that can be used to challenge the validity of patents. In the past, you had to go to a federal court to do this. Now, you can do it in an administrative court within the patent office.

From 2013 to 2015, Congressman Bob Goodlatte was pushing the Innovation Act, which is anything but that. The idea is that if you're suing someone who's infringing your patent and you lose, you pay the other side's legal costs. There are other features of this that are problematic, but this particular one discourages an inventor from taking a big manufacturer to court because the inventor will wind up broke.

In 2013, the Obama White House brought out a study about the dangers to American innovation created by patent trolls, firms that buy patents and then sue operating companies. Recently, the Supreme Court, in the *Alice Corp.* decision, made it more difficult to enforce a patent on software. Under the Obama administration, the Antitrust Division of the Justice Department regularly threatened to use the antitrust laws against holders of what are called standard-essential patents. These are the patents that allow every cell phone to talk to every other cell phone, for example.

A colleague of mine and I decided to see how great the threat of patent trolls was to the innovation system. The total revenues of high-tech industries in the United States are $627 billion a year. The litigation costs plus the revenues of patent trolls amount to roughly 1 percent of that figure. That's an upper-bound measure. It's very hard to maintain that the innovation economy is threatened by an industry, the patent troll industry, whose total revenues and litigation costs are less than what Americans spend on Halloween every year. We spend $7 billion on Halloween (of which $365 million is on pet costumes).

Who's running the anti-patent movement? I'm doing some research with a young colleague on this, and the answer is that it's a very small group of very big tech companies that would like to pay less for patents held by small inventors and small firms than they would otherwise. Google, it turns out, has been an extremely active lobbyist in this area; not only has Google spent large sums, but it also placed large numbers of former Google employees, and lawyers who have represented Google, in the Obama White House.

In short, the bottom line is this: if you take away the intellectual property rights, you take away innovation, wealth, and the ability to influence world events—the very things that make America exceptional.

PART TWO

American Exceptionalism and the Economy

5

The Exceptional Economy

EDWARD P. LAZEAR

When I was a young child, my father used to emphasize to me that, in America, we were all individuals and could do anything we desired. America was the land of opportunity. But while most coming-of-age Americans may have heard such sentiments from their own parents, the message is not universal. When I conveyed my father's words to a European colleague, she said, "Oh, really? We were told exactly the opposite. Our parents always told us, 'Don't think you're so special. You're one of a large group of people in society, but you're not so special.'"

In an economic sense, are we special—or rather, is America exceptional? Part of the answer is revealed in tracing the relative growth of our GDP compared to other countries over time, starting in the 1820s. Unsurprisingly, our political parents, the British, once led the world in terms of GDP per capita. That has changed over time. We gradually matched the United Kingdom, eventually and significantly surpassing them after World War II. By 2010, we were 28 percent richer than Britain, 22 percent richer than our Canadian counterparts, and 65 percent richer than Italy.

When assessing the American economy, economists and noneconomists alike care first about whether the economy offers the prospect of a good living or healthy wages. A related concern is a desire for job security. Does our labor market offer us freedom from the worry that our source of income is in jeopardy? And finally, the third factor addresses the long-term wish that our children be able to live better than we do. We want our economy to afford continual opportunity, and we want our children to be upwardly mobile.

The American economy has done quite well in terms of both income levels and growth. What about job security? The unemployment rate is one measure of job security. Over the last thirty years, the unemployment rates in the United States, on average, have been lower than just about every comparable country in the world. The one exception to this statement is Japan. Japan has exceedingly low unemployment rates, and it is entirely reasonable to ask why we are not surpassing them in this metric. One possibility is that Japan's unemployment rate is actually too low. Japan has a somewhat stagnant, impacted labor force that may have too little labor market churn. The United States has low unemployment rates but also has one of the most dynamic labor forces in the world.

Most American children actually do better than their parents despite the rhetoric and fears to the contrary. According to a dataset called the Panel Study of Income Dynamics, 84 percent of children are earning more than their parents in real buying-power terms, which corrects for inflation.[1]

Ninety-three percent of children in the lowest quintile—that is, the people whose parents were in the bottom 20 percent—do better than their parents. That is not so surprising. It is easier to rise to the top when starting from the bottom. But even among the top 20 percent, 70 percent of children do better than their parents.

In terms of mobility, is it possible for Americans to move up, or are we stuck where we were born? The answer is that we move up very successfully. Of the people who are currently in the top 20 percent of earners in the United States, 60 percent came from families that were in quintiles other than the top 20 percent. If it were purely random, 80 percent would come from the other quintiles because 80 percent by definition are in the other four quintiles.

To be fair, America has been criticized for some lack of mobility across generations, and this is particularly true within certain communities, especially among the poorest individuals in our society. There is some tendency to get locked in. But most of income is not explained by birth, and that is not a strictly American phenomenon. For example, in Canada, the leader in mobility, 95 percent of income is not determined by parental income. Factors other than parents' income account for 95 percent of variation in personal income in that country.

In the United States, that figure is lower, but it's still 78 percent: the bulk of where you end up in the economy is independent of where you were born in terms of your income or your status. Despite the fact that we're not doing quite as well as some other countries in this measure, we actually do very well in terms of mobility albeit less well than some other countries.

The best indicator of whether we are exceptional is the market test. Are people buying our products? Do people want to come here? There are four times as many people in the queue for a green card as are actually issued one in any given year.[2] We are the team everybody wants to play for.

A survey of Europeans asked in which country respondents would prefer to work.[3] The largest number chose the United States. We do not see Russia or China on that list. We remain the choice destination. People are putting their money where their mouths are, and this tells us that the United States is exceptional.

What are the ingredients that have made our economy so successful over time? There are a number of factors. There are four clear factors: we are industrious; we are a mobile society; we are welcoming; and, compared with others, we have light regulation and low taxes.

Tocqueville wrote, "The state of things is without parallel in the history of the world. In America, everyone finds facilities unknown elsewhere for making or increasing this fortune, the spirit of gain is always eager, swayed by no other impulse but the pursuit of wealth." Tocqueville admired Americans' pursuit of wealth, an attribute that some view negatively these days.

Tocqueville was really affirming a position that was articulated decades earlier, in 1776, by Adam Smith in *The Wealth of Nations,* where he argued that people acting in their own interest will, like an invisible hand, help the economy grow and move things forward. Tocqueville had never seen a country that had people working to move this invisible hand along as successfully as in the United States.

That remains true. We work harder than our counterparts. Figure 1 shows the average number of hours worked per person in the working-age population.[4] This is not merely the average number of hours worked among workers. It takes the total number of hours that people are working and divides that number by the population, so having a large percentage of our population employed is one reason why our average hours of work among those who can work is so high.

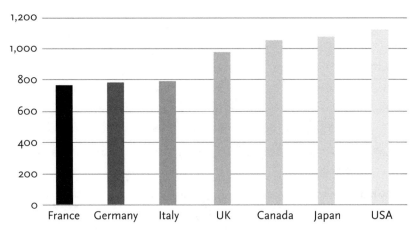

Figure 1. Average Hours Worked Annually per Person, 1991–2014

Japan used to lead in this regard for a significant period after World War II. But in the last couple of decades, the United States has passed Japan. We have both high labor force participation and hours of work. Some may believe we are working ourselves to death. But I view it positively. Wealth has not made us lazy. We still seem to have the drive that was required to make the economy and the country grow throughout our first two hundred years.

We also work hard in school. We invest very heavily in education and human capital. Not only is it true that we lead the big countries in terms of average levels of schooling right now, but we did so early on. We had compulsory schooling up to age sixteen before almost all the other countries in the world did. We recognize the value of education and of investing in human capital, and we were willing to put resources behind that view.

Education is an important driver of geographic mobility, and there our numbers are impressive. In any given year, 16 percent of the US population has moved, compared to 7 percent in the European Union.[5] If a good job comes up on the other side of the country, Americans are willing to take it. Europeans historically have been less likely to move. And geographic mobility is an important determinant of economic growth. When I was growing up here, California had 10 million people. It now has three and a half times that. It still has very rapid expansion, manifesting a mobility westward from the east. There were tremendous opportunities on the West Coast, and Americans moved to take advantage of them.

An example of another kind of mobility that was extremely important in the development of this country is the migration of African Americans from the rural South to the urban North, which took place starting in the late 1940s and continued throughout the 1980s and 1990s. Cities such as Detroit, which started out with very low African American populations, became very highly African American, in large part because of economic opportunities in manufacturing. More recently, we have seen the reverse: mobility back down to the urban South, adding to the growth of cities such as Dallas, Houston, Miami, and Atlanta. This is an exceptional American phenomenon.

In addition to geographic mobility, we enjoy job mobility. In any given year, about 60 million people are hired, which is two-fifths of the labor force. At the same time, 58 million are separated. Labor market churn helps move workers to their most productive use. We lead the world in this type of mobility. Ten years ago, a colleague and I did a book in which we looked at a dozen countries and compared this labor-force mobility. Some other countries also do fairly well in this respect. Denmark, surprisingly, is a very mobile and quite open labor market. We are the leaders.

America is exceptional in the opportunities it offers immigrants. Of all countries, including Canada, we are the only one where the unemployment rate among the foreign born is lower than that among the native born. Our immigrants actually do better in finding jobs than does the native-born population. We remain a welcoming nation.

This good news is related to our relatively light labor regulation. Employment at will essentially implies that the employer is free to decide whether or not you work for that firm. This is less true in Europe, where layoffs cannot happen without compensation. That seemingly just approach has consequences. In Spain, for instance, employers have to give a laid-off employee six months of pay if they are laid off after ten years of service. In Italy, it's about $2,000 for three years of service. As a reaction to that, firms in these countries have lowered their hiring rates dramatically. If a company fears that it cannot lay off a worker, it is less likely to hire in the first place.

As a result, European companies have moved toward temporary employment contracts. In France today, virtually everyone is hired into a temporary job. People who stay in the jobs for long enough become permanent, and this frequently results in inefficient termination. Just when the worker is getting good at the job, he is terminated so the employer does not have to make him a permanent employee.

America has also had historically light taxes. The ratio of combined state, local, and federal tax to GDP in the United States is 26 percent. In France, the figure is 45 percent.[6] By international standards, our taxes are still quite low.

There are also less quantitative elements that differentiate our economy from other economies in the world. We are much less tolerant of economic class welfare than most economies. We do not have labor parties in the United States. Socialism has never taken off here. Even the union movement in the United States is thought of as one of business unionism, as opposed to social or revolutionary unionism.

Sam Gompers, the founder of the American Federation of Labor, said he believed that management and workers could get together to reach beneficial understandings—to get the job done with a fair day's work for a fair day's pay. Other countries have revolutionary unionism, which is essentially the desire to displace, rather than work with, capitalists.

Finally, new money tends to dominate old money in this country. The Fortune 500 firms in 1955 did not include McDonald's, Walmart, Apple, CVS, Microsoft, Amazon, Home Depot, or United Health Group. All these firms are now among the top twenty firms in the country, with a number in the top ten. None of these firms existed in 1955.

The same is true of individual wealth. A hundred years ago, the group of richest families in the country consisted of well-known names such as Sloan, Carnegie, Ford, and Getty. Their descendants are probably still pretty wealthy, but the group of big names today is dominated by Buffett, Gates, Ellison, Bezos, Koch, Zuckerberg, Bloomberg, Walton, and Page—names that were unknown two or three decades ago.

Is this mobility a stable element of American economics, or has it changed over time? Consider President Obama's response to a question by Edward Luce of the *Financial Times* about whether America is exceptional. Obama said, "I believe in American exceptionalism just as I suspect the Brits believe in British exceptionalism and the Greeks believe in Greek exceptionalism." That was a very tactful answer, but this is probably not the topic on which we want our president to be humble. It is not such a bad thing for the president of the United States to believe that we are the greatest country in the world, especially given evidence that supports that view.

Indeed, there was some erosion under President Obama in those factors that make America exceptional. Obama did not subscribe to the view that light regulation is beneficial. Nor did he seem to believe that incentives matter very much, emphasizing redistribution over growth as the most important feature in an economy, labeling growing inequality and lack of upward mobility the defining challenges of our times. We have seen in recent years the erosion of employment at will, and we have seen rising marginal tax rates.

During the Obama administration we saw increased regulation—the Dodd-Frank Act, the Affordable Care Act, aggressive action by the Environmental Protection Agency, and the Department of the Interior's redefinition of navigable waters, among the most egregious. These moves may undermine the exceptionalism that has characterized the past two centuries.

Exceptionalism is not all about economics. While it is true that economic success affects our standard of living, it also affects our prominence in the world. Historically, the countries that have led the world politically tend to be the richest. It is expensive to have an army. It is expensive to have national defense. It is expensive to be a world leader. Consider ancient Rome, eighteenth-century Britain, and the United States in the twentieth century. All were at the time of prominence the richest economies in the world. The Soviet Union collapsed when it became impoverished and could no longer afford to support an enormous military. Russia's self-confidence and desire to affect its neighbors seem to vary with the price of oil, which is a significant source of government revenue. Similarly, China's recent aggressiveness in the South China Sea and elsewhere in the world matches its economic progress. Whether we want to be a world power is a separate matter. But having the ability to do so clearly depends on our exceptional economic position. If we lose it, we will be losing more than merely the right to claim that we are the land of opportunity.

Notes

1. Pew Charitable Trusts, *Pursuing the American Dream: Economic Mobility across Generations,* 2012, 4, http://pewtrusts.org/~/media/legacy/uploadedfiles/pcs_assets/2012/pursuingamericandreampdf.pdf (accessed June 8, 2017).

2. U.S. Department of State, Bureau of Consular Affairs, "Annual Immigrant Visa Waiting List Report as of November 1, 2015," 2015; and Department of Homeland Security, Office of Immigration Statistics, "Yearbook of Immigration Statistics 2014," 2016.

3. European Commission, "Geographical and Labour Market Mobility: Report," Special Eurobarometer 337, June 2010, 32, http://ec.europa.eu/public_opinion/archives/ebs/ebs_337_en.pdf (accessed June 8, 2017).

4. Organization for Economic Co-operation and Development, Statistical Data Base, 1991–2014, http://stats.oecd.org (accessed June 8, 2017).

5. Alexander Janiak and Etienne Wasmer, *Mobility in Europe—Why It Is Low, the Bottlenecks and the Policy Solutions,* European Commission, 2008, 22.

6. Organization for Economic Co-operation and Development, Centre for Tax Policy and Administration, https://oecd.org/ctp (accessed June 8, 2017).

6

Law and the Regulatory State

JOHN COCHRANE

To be a conservative—or, as in my case, an empirical, Pax-Americana, rule-of-law, constitutionalist, conservative libertarian—is pretty much by definition to believe that America is "exceptional"—and that it is perpetually in danger of losing that precious characteristic. Exceptionalism is not natural or inborn but must be understood, cherished, maintained, and renewed each generation—and its garden is always perilously unattended.

Like every word describing beliefs, however, "exceptionalism" is a slippery concept. America's detractors often use the same word pejoratively and derisively. To them, exceptionalism means a parochial and ignorant moral superiority. We are not the first or only society to see itself as exceptional, different, or somehow better than everyone else.

The Promise

So why *is* America exceptional, in the good sense? Here, I think, economics provides a crucial answer. The ideas that American exceptionalism propounds have led to the most dramatic improvement in widely shared well-being in human history. That improvement is not just material but includes health, life span, peace, and any measure of human prosperity. Yes, despite the horrors we read about from the world's war zones and some of our own cities, violence remains on a steady decline.

Aesop tells of a hungry wolf who meets and admires a well-fed dog. But when the wolf sees the dog's collar, he says "no thanks" and walks off. Fortunately, we do not face the wolf's conundrum. We do not have to argue for a moral superiority of freedom and ask for material sacrifice. In the United States it is possible to be both well fed and free.

Despite the promises of monarchs, autocrats, dictators, commissars, central planners, socialists, industrial policy makers, progressive nudgers, and assorted dirigistes, it is liberty and rule of law that has led to this enormous progress. To the Chinese argument, say, that their ancient culture demands authoritarianism, a simple reply suffices: you, $7,000 per capita GDP and filthy air; us, $52,000 per capita and a clean environment.

I do not think this outcome was intentional. Neither the Founders, nor those who built the British institutions that the Founders improved, had any idea of the material progress their invention would father, or that the United States would rise to lead the world to a seventy-year Pax Americana. Jefferson envisioned a bucolic agrarian society. Washington warned against foreign entanglements. A system designed only to defend individual liberty unintentionally unleashed unimaginable material and international benefits.

Without this economic success, I doubt that anyone would call America exceptional. Imagine that China were seven times as productive per capita as we are, rather than the other way around. Or imagine that great natural experiment, North Korea versus South Korea had the reverse outcome. North Korea also claims to be exceptional. The rest of the world regards it as an exceptional basket case.

Of course, the foundations of this prosperity—in rule of law, security of property, internal peace—are not ours alone. America was built on British institutions. Other countries have adopted many of our institutions and joined in our prosperity.

In fact, the core of exceptionalist faith contains its own undoing. If American values are indeed universal, if America's exceptional role is to bring these ideas to the world, then when the world does adopt these ideas, America must become somewhat less exceptional.

America is already less *unusual* than it was at its founding and throughout the eras of monarchy, of dictatorship, and of Soviet communism when America's detractors insisted it would be just one more short-lived republic. But the process is far from over. The United States remains the essential exceptional nation.

All the great ideas for the next advances in human well-being are being made here: computers and the Internet, biotech, genetics, the microbiome. Most important, the great ideas are being *implemented* here—the new companies are American.

More darkly, any hope for resolving the world's gathering storm clouds resides in the United States. If we *don't* get our act together and revive our exceptionalism, and pretty darn soon, the consequences are truly terrifying: chaos in the Middle East; more swarms of refugees; Russian and Chinese forcible expansion; nuclear weapons going off here and there; pandemics among people, animals, or crops, which often follow waves of globalization. The troops in the First Iraq War wore T-shirts saying, "Who you gonna call? 001." It's still the only number.

Enough self-congratulation—it's time to move on to the second item of a conservative's faith: that it's all in danger of falling apart. And it is, more than ever.

The Rule of Law

I locate the core source of America's exceptional nature in our legal system—the nexus of constitutional government, artfully created with checks and balances, and of the rule of law that guides our affairs. And this is also where I locate the greatest danger at the moment.

Lawyers? Government? You chuckle. That you may laugh just tells us how endangered this precious flower is. Without rule of law, any American character fostering innovation is quickly squashed.

Rule of law means the rights of the accused to know charges against them, to see evidence, to confront witnesses; the right of free speech and especially unwelcome political speech; the separation of prosecution and judges; grand juries to weigh evidence and grant warrants for searches; the right to property and courts that will defend what that right means (fracking developed in the United States pretty much because property rights include subsoil minerals, which are retained by the government in most other countries); the delicate constitutional checks and balances that keep majorities from running amok and delay awful ideas until enthusiasm passes; a free press that can expose corruption; and so on, ad infinitum.

Even democracy only lives on top of rule of law. We are a republic, not a democracy, and for good reasons. Democracy is fundamentally a check on tyranny, not a good way to run day-to-day public affairs. Democracy without rule of law produces neither prosperity nor freedom. Even countries like Venezuela and Russia go through the motions of elections, but you can't get a building permit there without connections or speak out against the government without losing your job. On the other hand, rule of law without democracy can function for a time and tends to produce democracy. America lived for 150 years under rule of law while still a monarchy.

And without rule of law, democracy is soon subverted. Those in government are always tempted to use the government's power to silence opposition and cement their hold on power, and ruin the economy in the process. *That's* the danger we face. If speaking out for a candidate, arguing a policy question such as climate change, or working on behalf of a losing party earns you the tender attentions of the Securities and Exchange Commission (SEC), Internal Revenue Service (IRS), Environmental Protection Agency (EPA), Consumer Financial Protection Bureau (CFPB), National Labor Relations Board (NLRB), and increasingly the Department of Justice (DOJ) and the Federal Bureau of Investigation (FBI), it does not matter who votes.

Erosion of Rule of Law

The erosion of rule of law is all around us. I see it most clearly in the explosion of the administrative, regulatory state. Most of the "laws" we face are not, in fact, laws, written by a legislature and signed by an executive, as we are taught in school. They are regulations, promulgated by agencies. This system made sense, initially. For example, it does not make sense for Congress to write the criteria for maintaining an airliner. But now it has spiraled out of control. The Affordable Care Act (Obamacare) and the Dodd-Frank Act (banking regulation) are poster children. Their enabling acts go on for thousands of pages. The subsidiary regulations go on for tens of thousands. The letters and statements of interpretation and guidance, now essentially laws of their own, go on for more.

Were these even rules that one could read and comply with, the situation wouldn't be so bad. But the real problem is that the rules are so vague and complex that nobody knows what they really mean. Companies can't just read a set of written rules. They must ask for regulator approval, which can take years and yields arbitrary results. Hence, the "rules" really just mean discretion for the regulators to do what they want—often to coerce the behavior they want out of companies by the threat of an arbitrary adverse decision. Anyone can be found guilty at any time—if a regulator chooses to single someone out, as an EPA administrator once said, for "crucifixion."

Richard Epstein calls the system "government by waiver." The law and regulations are impossible to comply with. So business after business asks for waivers, which are granted, mostly. But you'd be out of your head to object too loudly to the actions of an agency or the administration it serves if you want a waiver.

On top of laws, rules, and judicial interpretations, now agencies write "guidance" letters to state their interpretation of a rule, and these letters become law themselves.

As with laws, agencies promulgating new regulations are supposed to follow a procedure. They are supposed to respect and implement Congress's authorizing legislation, incorporate public comment, perform serious cost-benefit analysis, and so forth. But even these weak constraints are less and less binding.

Obamacare subsidies, the Federal Trade Commission's regulation of the Internet, the EPA's assault on carbon and coal, the obstruction of the Keystone XL pipeline, the Department of Education's war on private colleges, the Federal Deposit Insurance Corporation's withdrawal of bank access from payday lenders and pot farmers: all of these step far outside the established procedural limits. (My point is not about the merits of any of these examples, which may be fine regulations. My point is the lack of rule-of-law process in how they were promulgated.)

The basic rights that citizens are supposed to have in the face of the law are also vanishing in the regulatory state. The agency is prosecutor, judge, jury, appeals court, executioner, and recipient of fine money all rolled into one. One does not have conventional rights to see evidence and calculations, discover information, and challenge witnesses. Agencies change their interpretation of the law and come after their victims ex post facto.

Retroactive decisions are common, never mind the constitutional prohibition on bills of attainder. When the DOJ and CFPB went after auto lenders, based on a statistical analysis of last names of people who had received auto loans, the computer program was obviously not announced ahead of time, so businesses had no idea whether or not they were following the law. The CFPB went after PHH, a mortgage lender, issuing a novel interpretation of the law, charging PHH ex post facto with violation of that new interpretation, and increasing its own administrative judge's $6 million fine to $109 million.

The expansion of the regulatory state, along with the disappearance of rule of law in its operation, is already having its economic impact. The long-term growth rate of the US economy has been cut in half, a decrease driven largely by anemic investment.

I fear even more the political impact. The point of rule of law is to keep government from using law for political purposes. As we lose rule of law in the regulatory state, its politicization is inevitable. Recall Lois Lerner of the IRS and her treatment of conservative groups. Recall Governor Scott Walker's persecution by Wisconsin's attorney general using vague campaign finance laws.

The drive toward criminalizing regulatory witch hunts and going after the executives means one thing: those executives had better make sure their organizations stay in line. ITT Technical Institute got closed down as part of the Obama administration's war on for-profit education. Laureate International Universities, the for-profit college that coincidentally paid Bill Clinton $17.6 million for being "honorary chancellor," did not. The SEC is piling onto an ambitious state-attorneys-general drive to sue Exxon, under securities law, for insufficient piety over climate change. Big "settlements" with banks are leading to millions of dollars being channeled to left-wing and Democratic Party political-advocacy groups.

The classic analysis of regulation says it leads to capture: the industry captures the regulator, they get cozy, and regulation ends up being used to stifle competition in the industry. Capture is now going the other way. Health insurers, banks, and energy companies are slowly being captured by the politicized regulators. Yes, they still get protection, but they must do the regulators' and administrations' political bidding. And a constant stream of CEO show trials and criminal investigations keeps them in line—with calls for more. Just imagine what they could do with lists of donors to out-of-power party political action committees and nonprofits.

Campaign finance law is precisely about regulating speech and the government taking control over who can support whom in an election. Corporations will be forced to disclose contributions. Unions will not.

The key attribute that makes America exceptional—and prosperous—is that *candidates and their supporters can afford to lose elections.* Grumble, sit back, regroup, and try again next time. They won't lose their jobs or their businesses. They won't suddenly encounter trouble getting permits and approvals. They won't have alphabet soup agencies at their doors with investigations and fines. They won't have prosecutions of their political associations. We are losing that attribute.

In many countries, people can't afford to lose elections. Those in power do not give it up easily. Those out of power are reduced to violence. American exceptionalism does not mean that all the bad things that happen elsewhere in the world cannot happen here.

Perhaps I am guilty of nostalgia, but I sense that, once upon a time, those in American public life believed that their first duty was to keep alive the beautiful structure of American government, and the policy passion of the day came second and within that constraint.

We are suffering now a devotion to outcome, to winning the battle of the moment at any cost. Legislation that passes by one vote? Fine. Regulations written far past enabling authority? Go for it. Executive order in place of law or regulation? Do it. Just write a letter of interpretation to tell them what to do. Shove it down their throats. But when policies are adopted without at least grudging consensus that the battle was fairly won, you can't afford to lose an election.

Since the Nixon impeachment, and with the spread of campaign finance law and regulation, we are seeing a greater and greater "criminalization of politics." It's part of the trend toward using any tool to win. And it is more and more dangerous to lose an election, so those in power will fight by any means to hang on.

Our public life depends on voluntary cooperation. Administrations follow the law, even when they don't really have to. They defer to court and Supreme Court decisions that they could ignore. The president does have a pen and a phone—and the number at DOJ and FBI and IRS. The rule of law depends on him not using it. We do not ask the question too insistently, "So, what are you going to do about it?" We are losing that respect for the system.

The idea of rule of law, the reverence for process over outcome, seems to be disappearing. Few college seniors will have any idea what we're talking about. Even basic civics courses are passé. And we see so much on both sides of the partisan divide that ignores it. Our many foreign policy misadventures have a common theme: forgetting that all societies need rule-of-law foundations, not just the superficial exercise of voting.

Rule of law, then, depends on a culture that respects it, not just the written word. And that culture depends on people to some extent understanding how it works. Like medieval peasants, having lost the recipe, looking up in awe at Roman concrete structures, I fear, our children will wonder just how the architecture of a broken system once worked its marvels. And the Romans lasted a thousand years. Pax Americana seems to be running out of steam at a mere 250.

Egalitarianism and the Pursuit of Happiness

Our government's purpose is set forth in the Declaration of Independence: to secure "life, liberty, and the pursuit of happiness," period. Government does not exist to lead us to some grander purpose: the advancement of the Christian faith or the restoration of the Caliphate; the spread of communism on earth; propounding the greatness of our kultur or the glorious American nation. When John F. Kennedy said, "Ask not what your country can do for you—ask what you can do for your country," he had it precisely wrong.

Yes, American exceptionalists wish to spread their ideas to the world, but not to subjugate other people to some greater cause, instead merely to allow them to pursue life, liberty, and happiness as those people see it.

A central article of exceptionalist faith is that American institutions are universal. We deny that they are specific to a culture or race. People everywhere want freedom and can learn to use American institutions to get it as quickly as they can learn to use an American iPhone to order American pizza (sorry, Italy!).

Most of all, government does not exist to further the ethnic or religious identity of a people. Throughout the world, governments parcel up the spoils of power along ethnic and religious lines. Each losing ethnic or religious group then needs its own government to defend its simple economic and expressive rights. Multicultural and multiethnic empires have existed before. But by and large they were empires of tolerance, not right, and extracted resources from citizens equally rather than serving them equally.

In the United States, the children of Serbians and Croatians, of Indians and Pakistanis, of Catholics and Protestants and Muslims and Jews, live side by side and intermarry. None imagine that they need a government run by one of their own ethnic group or religion for basics like getting a business permit. The idea that government serves to foster their ethnic or religious identity becomes quickly foreign. Yes, this melting pot ideal has never been perfect, but it holds much more here than in any other country.

But how quaint this melting pot view seems now!

Interestingly, that ideal disappeared first from our foreign policy. For a hundred years, the United States has stood behind ethnic or religious governments, happily playing one against the other and not once say-ing, "You know, we have a better idea for managing this, one where you won't be at each other's throats for another century or so."

But that exceptional ideal is now vanishing domestically as well. Our government requires us to fill out forms with fine racial categorizations. The core principle that to be treated fairly by the law you do not need to be represented by a police officer, mayor, member of Congress, senator, or president of your own particular racial, ethnic, or religious identity is not only fading away but its opposite is enshrined in law.

It is true that these measures stemmed from the overturning of the even more egregious violation of American principles in laws governing African Americans, not only in the Jim Crow South but the segregated North as well. But at least we paid lip service to the principle.

A country that believes, and enshrines in law, the principle—opposed to everything in American exceptionalism—that you cannot be treated fairly by a government unless the officials of that government share your exact racial, ethnic, religious, and soon gender identity will fracture.

Similarly, exceptional America does not recognize the concept of "class." Our disavowal of aristocracy and titles set us distinctly apart from Britain in the nineteenth century. And yet we now use that language all the time—"middle class" or "working class" especially. Economic law, regulation, and policy increasingly treat income as a per-manent class designator, as fine and permanent as Indian castes, and treat citizens on that basis every bit as much as monarchic Britain treated peasants differently from nobles. We decry the reduction in mixing in America, yet when housing, food, medicine, and so on are distributed based on income, income becomes a permanent class marker.

Opportunity is a key part of the egalitarian credo. But a society div-vied up by formal categories of class, race, and income quickly loses that opportunity. As with economic regulation, though, each such division is a client usefully exploited for political advantage. Exceptional Amer-ica foreswore the opportunistic politics of such divisions.

Fixing America

The third article in exceptionalist faith, however, is optimism: that despite the ever-gathering clouds, America will once again face the challenge and reform. There is a reason that lovers of liberty tend to be Chicago Cubs fans. (And, as a member of both tribes, I take hope from one for the other!)

Healing is not something we should take for granted, however. There is no automatic self-correcting force. Every scrape with disaster is a scrape with disaster. It can happen here. Hope is not a strategy.

The recipe is straightforward. Rather than just demand "less regulation" even louder, we need to bring rule-of-law *process and protections* to the regulatory state and revive them in our legal procedures as well. It's time to pay attention to the *structure* of government rather than to its *outcome*.

Congress should restructure the law surrounding regulation. Stop writing thousand-page bills. Strengthen the Administrative Procedure Act describing how regulations are written and implemented. Require serious, and retrospective, cost-benefit analysis. Put in "shot clocks," time limits for regulatory decisions. Give people more avenues with which to challenge regulation in a timely manner. Sunset all regulations—they have to be reapproved (including congressional overview) and rewritten de novo every ten years.

Good news: people on both sides of the partisan divide recognize this fact. Paul Ryan's "Better Way" plan contains just this kind of radical restructuring of the regulatory process. It goes so far as to require that Congress must approve new major regulations—a large change in the balance of power back to Congress and away from administration and agencies. The Obama administration tried to strengthen the OIRA (Office of Information and Regulatory Affairs). The effort failed, but it signaled a bipartisan realization that the regulatory state is broken, and it taught some useful lessons.

The court system plays a crucial role. Fix the court system so litigants are not bankrupt and dead by the time they win. The litmus test for new judges should be their willingness to sustain rule-of-law restrictions on the regulatory state, not to refight social issues. Let the litmus test be *Wickard v. Filburn*, which declared that a man may not grow wheat in his own yard to make his own bread without a Federal Wheat Marketing Order, not *Roe v. Wade*.

A Small Comment on Foreign Policy

I have focused on economics, but nowhere is the decline of American exceptionalism more evident than in foreign policy. Post–World War II Pax Americana has been the most peaceful and prosperous period in all human history. But its development and success have been one narrow scrape after another, and in any of them things could have gone wrong. In the next one they may.

What country can look at the experience of Ukraine—to which the United States guaranteed territorial integrity in exchange for giving up nuclear weapons—of North Korea, Pakistan, Libya, and Iran and not conclude that getting nuclear weapons and rattling them is a darn good idea?

Teddy Roosevelt said to speak softly and to carry a big stick. America these days speaks loudly, aims at the daily polls, doesn't mean what it says, and announces ahead of time that it won't use its stick. Dwight Eisenhower did not tell Hitler ahead of time how many troops he was going to put in at Normandy and how quickly he would take them out. The answer was that he was going to put in enough to win, period.

The Bush administration gave the project of bringing democracy to the world a bad name, in part by misunderstanding just how much rule of law must underpin democracy and in part by misunderstanding just how much the world still needs the idea and culture of rule of law.

For a messianic, universalist religion, we do precious little missionary work these days.

Hope

It is common to bemoan the state of American politics. But we should be optimistic. The major parties are blowing up. We are in a once-in-a-generation major realignment and redefinition. Only a big realignment can produce the rule-of-law and free-market coalition that I describe here. Power may shift from the once imperial presidency to an emboldened Congress. Only a time of big change offers big opportunity.

Finally, ideas matter. An exceptional—and functional—America must understand how she is supposed to work. We are a democracy, and if voters don't respond with an elemental understanding of their rights, and with outrage when those rights are violated, as the Founders did, we can't expect miracle politicians to save us.

How can we expect our children to understand the machinery if we don't tell them? The schools and universities don't do that anymore. But other institutions do!

This book is the product of an exceptionally American institution, a reservoir of *ideas defining a free society*. Sometimes that reservoir is an ark, keeping ideas alive in a dark age. Sometimes it is a fountain, ready to bring those ideas to the world when it's ready. But you, I, and the institutions we form—another brilliantly exceptional American habit—are crucial to its renewal.

7

Whither American Exceptionalism?

NIALL FERGUSON

When you give an essay a title like "Whither American exceptionalism?" there is obviously a joke to be made. Is American exceptionalism withering? That is really the question that I want to pose.

Let me first talk a little bit about economic and political history, and tell you what has not been exceptional about American history. Let us look at population figures since the time of the early republic (see figure 1); the gray line is the population of the United States. The x-axis is on a logarithmic scale so that we can fit China in. This story is a clear-cut one. The population of the United States grew very rapidly. It overtook that of the European superpowers, the United Kingdom and Germany. It overtook that of Japan, one of the first Asian superpowers. It has just overtaken that of the former Soviet Union, and it is conceivable that one day it will overtake that of China.

This is remarkable, no doubt, but it is not especially exceptional. Economically, the story of American gross domestic product is remarkable, too (see figure 2). Once again, the gray line is the gross domestic

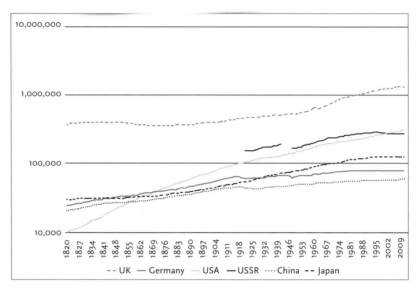

Figure 1. Populations of Modern Superpowers (Thousands, Log. Scale)

Source: Angus Maddison, *Historical Statistics of the World Economy: 1–2008 AD* (published online).

Note: For Germany, figures for 1820 to 1913 refer to the territory of the German Reich's 1913 boundaries (excluding Alsace–Lorraine). Figures for 1950 onward refer to 1991 frontiers. For USSR, figures refer to the territory of the Soviet Union, including the periods before and after its existence. For reference, the Russian Federation in 2009 accounted for just under half the population of the former Soviet Union, and 57 percent of the GDP.

product of the United States. Once again, I am comparing it with other historical superpowers. What you see here is the extraordinary story of American economic growth: outpacing the European great powers and from the late nineteenth century overtaking the United Kingdom; then dominating the global economy of the twentieth century. Notice the dotted line representing China, which since the 1980s has been closing the gap with the United States. The trajectory of its recent rise is almost vertical. For that reason alone, you cannot really say that American economic growth has been historically exceptional. It has been impressive, but once again it is not unique.

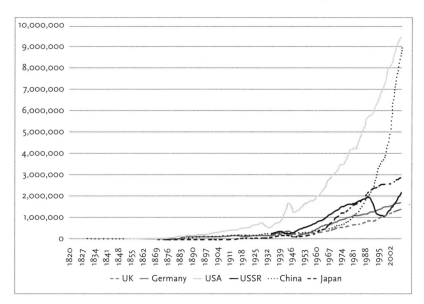

Figure 2. GDP of Modern Superpowers (Million 1990 International Dollars)

Source and note: as for figure 1.

Rapidly growing population, rapid economic growth—not to mention territorial expansion—and the global power that comes with these things were consequences of what was exceptional about the United States. The consequences themselves were not exceptional. There are other ways to achieve these things, and other great powers have achieved them in the past and may do so again in the future.

Now, if I were to ask a well-educated American, "What are the exceptional causes of American success?" she might very well reply by mentioning the fact that we are a democracy, or the fact that we are a republic and got rid of a bad British king. She might say, "We have a federal system," or "We have a capitalist economy." Yet none of these things is exceptional. Successful democracies are ten a penny. There have been successful republics since ancient times. The Dutch created

73

the United Provinces before rebellious British colonists here created the United States. Federal systems are also now commonplace. Even the Germans now have a federal system; indeed, they first had one when the German Reich was created in 1871. As for capitalist economies, these have become the default setting. So a story about American exceptionalism cannot be based on these political institutions, any more than it can be based on population growth or economic growth.

As a young man at Oxford, I was made to read Alexis de Tocqueville. I am very glad I was made to do that because Tocqueville remains for me the greatest and most insightful writer on the subject of American exceptionalism. I am going to take Tocquevillian ideas now—based not only on *Democracy in America* but also on his later work, *The Old Regime and the Revolution*—to suggest what I think is exceptional about the United States: in short, the characteristics that really are hard to find in other countries, in any era.

First, the idea of limited government, with the separation of powers designed to constrain both the executive and the legislature, was a highly original idea. British institutions were not designed this way. Second is the notion of decentralizing power. This was something that impressed Tocqueville very much as it was so different from his native France. Again, this is a highly original idea. Only in Switzerland do you otherwise find the notion of decentralization so fundamental to the political system. But as Tocqueville points out, American decentralization was about more than just giving local authorities and regional authorities power. It was also about giving voluntary associations power. The citizens do self-help in North America, he says, unlike anywhere else in the world.

Third, Tocqueville says that America puts liberty above equality. This is something he as a French aristocrat with liberal leanings greatly admired. Fourth—and I think this is one of the reasons that Tocqueville was critical about some of the things that he saw in the United States, not least the institution of slavery, but also the treatment of indigenous peoples—American citizenship ultimately evolved to be a universal citizenship based on norms, not on genes. In Tocqueville's time this was very far from being a reality. In our time, it has become a reality. I am going to add a fifth characteristic, which was also very important to Tocqueville: the vitality of American religious life—not only its vitality but its diversity. The competition between multiple Protestant sects, and then the competition with Catholicism as Catholics began to immigrate to the United States, have been among the key sources of American vitality.

These are the characteristics that I think were exceptional about the United States—characteristics that are very hard to find in the history of other countries. I happen to believe that these are the characteristics that explain not only the political success of the United States, and not only its economic success, but ultimately also its success as a great power.

Is American exceptionalism withering? Let me show you some of the symptoms that might lead you to conclude that it is. Take median household income (see figure 3). After 1999, following decades of growth, it steeply declined, and it has only barely got back into the range that we attained in the late 1990s. Compared with the trajectory for the year of my birth, 1964, up to 1999, we appear to have entered a period when, for the average American household, economic life has been a disappointing round-trip through a crisis into a mediocre recovery. Productivity growth, once at the core of American economic success, has also slumped since the new millennium began.

Or take labor force participation. When you look at prime-age males (men aged between twenty-five and fifty-four), the United States is now an outlier. No other developed country has seen such a sharp decline in prime-age male labor force participation. Nor is that all. The most shocking paper published in 2016, which was by Nobel laureate Angus Deaton and Anne Case, revealed sharply deteriorating health among middle-aged white Americans. Everybody else in the developed world, including nonwhite Americans, has a downward trajectory in terms of

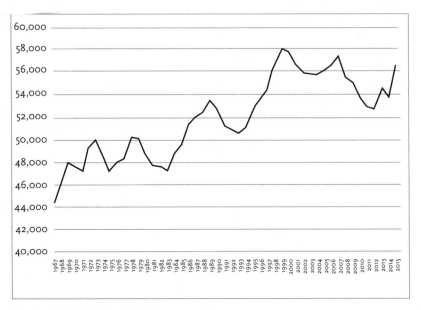

Figure 3. Median Household Income, 1967–2015

Source: U.S. Census Bureau, Current Population Survey, 1968 through 2016 Annual Social and Economic Supplements.
    Note: Calculated in 2015 inflation-adjusted (CPI-U-RS) dollars.

mortality. Only white middle-aged non-Hispanic Americans have an upward trajectory. And when you look at mortality by cause for this group, it is astonishing. Death by poisoning—that is, various forms of overdose—has been soaring, as have suicides and chronic liver diseases.[1]

Something is badly amiss with middle America, as Deaton and Case clearly show. But this should not really be news. Aspects of this social crisis were already identified in Charles Murray's wonderful book *Coming Apart*—a book that in some ways was a sociological prophecy of the Trump political phenomenon—as well as in *Hillbilly Elegy* by J. D. Vance.[2]

In the same way, when mathematical attainment among the children and grandchildren of professionals and managers is inferior to the mathematical attainment of Chinese children whose parents are manual workers, you know that we have a problem in education, too. The work that Raj Chetty has done at Stanford, as well as formerly at Harvard, shows that America has a new exceptionalism: the exceptionalism of failing schools and the exceptionalism of underachievement in education.[3]

All these things help us understand why the world is catching up. Figure 4 shows the ratio of American per capita GDP to Chinese per capita GDP.

At peak, Americans were twenty-two times richer than the Chinese. That was in the late 1970s, before the Chinese began their economic reforms. Now, Americans are less than five times richer. The "great divergence" that was the big story of economic history in the eighteenth, nineteenth, and twentieth centuries has reversed itself, and we are living through a great re-convergence. Indeed, by one measure, which is gross

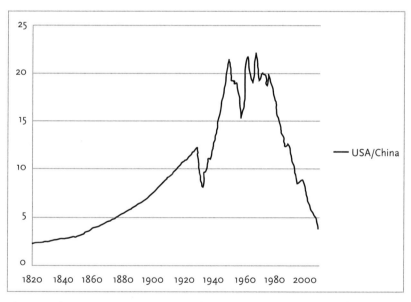

Figure 4. The Great Divergence: Ratio of Per Capita GDP, 1820–2010

Source: as for figure 1.

domestic product adjusted for purchasing power parity, China's aggregate GDP overtook that of the United States some years ago.

We would therefore not be wrong if we concluded that something is wrong, perhaps something is even rotten, in the state of the United States. We would almost certainly be wrong, however, if we concluded that the problem was immigration. Why? Because, as figure 5 shows, immigration has still not returned to the levels it achieved in the late nineteenth century when 14 percent of the population was foreign-born. The late nineteenth century was certainly a time of American overachievement. It is hard to believe that immigration, which was so crucial to the United States in the nineteenth century, has suddenly become toxic to it.

Other people blame inequality for America's problems. It is certainly true that, if one looks at income distribution before tax, the United

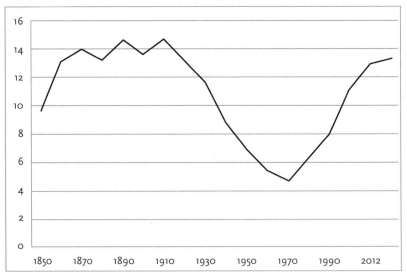

Figure 5. Foreign-Born Population as a Percentage of Total US Population, 1850–2014

Source: Table Ad354-443 in Susan B. Carter, Scott Sigmund Gartner, Michael R. Haines, Alan L. Olmstead, Richard Sutch, and Gavin Wright (eds.), *Historical Statistics of the United States, Earliest Times to the Present: Millennial Edition* (New York: Cambridge University Press, 2006), updated with data from the U.S. Census Bureau.

States has gone back to roughly where it was in the 1920s. But was the United States failing in the 1920s? On the contrary, it was the most innovative economy in the world. I am therefore skeptical of the argument that somehow inequality is to blame for the problems that I have just described to you.

In *The Great Degeneration,* a book I published in 2013, I made the argument that four things could explain why the United States was no longer performing exceptionally. One, there has been a fundamental breakdown of that contract between the generations that is at the heart of any political system. Two, our economy is increasingly enmeshed in a tangle of regulations. Three, the rule of law, which was once so central to the American system, has degenerated into the rule of lawyers. Four, that civil society based on voluntary associations about which Tocqueville wrote so eloquently has also degenerated.[4]

In other words, the problems that we see in the United States today—the problems that have generated what the rest of the world sees as a political crisis—are not the results of immigration, or inequality, or globalization, or even technology. The problems that we see, in my view, are the results of institutional decay. The institutions that made the United States exceptional are in a state of disrepair. We should not therefore be surprised by the symptoms of degeneration that we see in our economy, in our society, and indeed in our culture.

For years, my good friend Larry Kotlikoff has been pointing out that our fiscal system constitutes a massive fraud on future generations.[5] By estimating the net present value of all the federal government's income and all the federal government's expenditures, he works out what would have to be done to achieve generational balance today—in other words, what it would take to equalize the taxes paid and benefits received by this generation relative to future generations. The answer he arrives at is absolutely extraordinary. If such steps had been taken in 2013, all federal taxes would have been increased by 64 percent immediately and permanently, or all government outlays cut by a third. That is how out of kilter our fiscal system is. As long as we do not address it, the problem keeps getting worse. What this analysis implies, in essence, is that our current fiscal system condemns future generations either to much higher taxes or to much lower entitlements or to some combination of the two.

In previous eras, present generations sacrificed for posterity. My grandfathers fought in the world wars in the belief that they were making the world better for their children and grandchildren. In the postwar era, the baby boomers switched the transfer so that it now goes from posterity to them. The future, in other words, is making a huge sacrifice for the current generation. Edmund Burke brilliantly observed that the true social contract was between the dead, the living, and the unborn. In *The Great Degeneration* I argued that we have spectacularly breached that contract.

Figure 6 contrasts the gross domestic products of the United States, adjusted for inflation, with the size of the Federal Register, which is a compendium of all federal regulations, measured by total pages excluding any blank pages. Clearly, the size of the Federal Register has grown a great deal more rapidly than the size of our economy. Only in one presidency did the federal register shrink since the time of Franklin Roosevelt. Ronald Reagan remains the only president successfully to have reduced regulation since the 1930s.

As laws pile up, the legal system becomes more complicated. The more complicated things like the tax code are, the more subject they are to abuse. The more complicated the system, the more advantage goes to the big players, because they have the compliance departments and they have the lawyers. The same applies to the even larger volume of regulation that pours forth from the agencies of the "administrative state." The little guy—especially the small business owner—has the odds stacked against him.

Finally, let us consider associational life. In many ways, the Hoover Institution is itself a perfect example of the associational life that made America great. But each year the number of Americans who participate

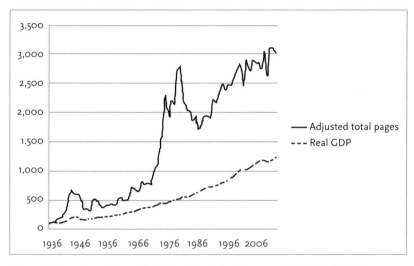

Figure 6. Number of Pages in Federal Register, Compared with Real GDP

Source: Clyde Wayne Crews Jr., *Ten Thousand Commandments: An Annual Snapshot of the Federal Regulatory State, 2013: 20th Anniversary Edition* (Washington, DC: Competitive Enterprise Institute, 2013).

Note: 1936 = 100.

in any kind of association, whether it is charitable, professional, environmental, or political, goes down. Figure 7 compares data from 1995 and 2006. If we had comparable data from a hundred years ago, it would be even clearer that we participate much less than we used to in what Tocqueville identified as the central American activity: doing things as citizens together rather than expecting the government to do them for us.

If Tocqueville were to come to the United States today and wander around the country, if he were to see the centralization of political power that has taken place, if he were to see the increasing complexity of our regulatory system, if he were to see how today's lawyers and judges behave, if he were to see the decline of associational life that has occurred in this country, then I am afraid he would be forced to conclude that the French at some point after his death had successfully invaded and taken over the United States of America.

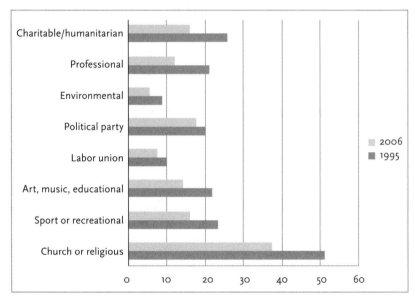

Figure 7. Active Membership of Voluntary Associations in the United States (1995 and 2006)

Source: World Values Survey Association, World Value Survey, 1981–2008, official aggregate v.20090902 (2009): www.wvsevsdb.com/wvs.

If American exceptionalism were a reality in 2016, then the United States would come top of league in tables like the annual survey which the World Economic Forum uses to calculate its economic competitiveness index. Table 1 shows twenty-two measures of institutional quality, ranging from the protection of private property rights to intellectual property rights, limits on corruption, the ethics of politicians, limits on bribery, and the independence of the judiciary. In not one single category does the United States come out on top.

Indeed, in most of these categories, the United States is somewhere in the middle of the pack. Take the cost of crime and violence. On that basis, the United States ranks 86th in the world and 87th when it

Issue	Top country	Top score	USA score	USA rank	Hong Kong rank
Property rights protected	Finland	6.5	5.0	42	7
Intellectual property rights protected	Finland	6.3	5.0	29	11
Limits on corruption	New Zealand	6.5	4.6	34	12
Politicians' ethics	Singapore	6.3	3.1	54	24
Limits on bribery	New Zealand	6.7	4.8	42	15
Independence of judiciary	New Zealand	6.7	4.9	38	12
No political favoritism	New Zealand	5.4	3.2	59	33
Efficiency of government spending	Singapore	6.0	3.2	76	17
Government regulation	Singapore	5.6	3.3	76	4
Efficiency of law in private disputes	Singapore	6.2	4.5	35	6
Efficiency of law in disputes with government	Finland	5.9	4.2	37	7
Transparency of govt. policy making	Singapore	6.2	4.4	56	4
Govt. help to improve business performance	Qatar	6.0	4.2	33	10
Low costs of terrorism	Slovenia	6.7	4.4	124	52
Low costs of crime and violence	Qatar	6.6	4.5	86	10
Low costs of organized crime	UAE	6.8	4.9	87	29
Reliability of police	Finland	6.6	5.5	29	17
Corporate ethics	New Zealand	6.6	5.0	29	17
Financial auditing and reporting standards	South Africa	6.6	5.2	37	10
Corporate governance	South Africa	5.8	5.1	23	28
Protection of minority shareholders	Finland	6.1	4.8	33	13
Investor protection	New Zealand	9.7	8.3	5	3

Table 1: Measures of the Rule of Law in the World Economic Forum's Annual Competitiveness Survey, 2011–2012

Source: World Economic Forum, Global Competitiveness Report, 2011–2012 (Geneva, 2011).

comes to the cost of organized crime. There is only one category where the United States is in the top ten of countries, and that is investor protection. So, where is American exceptionalism today? It is simply not visible in these data.

If you look at the indicators of governmental quality that the World Governance Institute publishes, you will see that in almost every measure—accountability, government effectiveness, regulatory quality, rule of law, control of corruption—the United States' scores have been going down since the 1990s, when this data set began (see figure 8). When you look at these data, you might be convinced that the United States is becoming a Latin American country—except that much of Latin America in the same period has seen improvement.

The right question we have to answer, in the light of all this evidence, is, can we make America exceptional again (as opposed to great again)? Nations can achieve greatness by all kinds of methods. The Russians

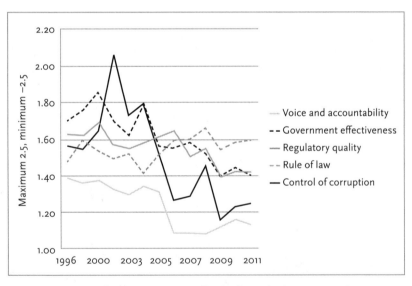

Figure 8. Estimates for Governance Quality, in the United States, 1996–2011

Source: World Justice Project, *Rule of Law Index 2011* (Washington, DC, 2011).

have shown that. The Chinese have shown it, too. Being great is definitely a distinct phenomenon from being good. But being exceptional is a different thing again. Can we make America exceptional again? I believe we can, because I think all the problems that I have described are essentially man-made and therefore fixable.

Public finance is a mess, but it is fixable. The long-range projections of the Congressional Budget Office show that, in terms of public debt as a share of GDP, the United States could well be Japan by midcentury (see figure 9). However, we can fix this in ways that are still within our reach—through tax reform and entitlement reform. If we simplified the tax code and addressed the entitlement imbalances, we could fix the fiscal crisis.

We can also reduce the burden of regulation. Certain sectors of our economy have become punitively regulated, and no president has increased regulation more since World War II than Barack Obama. But

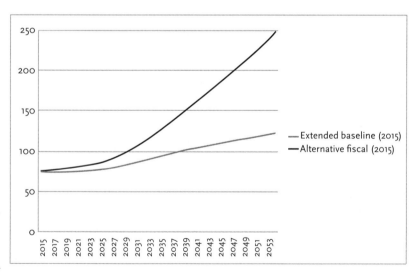

Figure 9. CBO Projections for Federal Debt Held by the Public as Percentage of GDP, 2015–2053

Source: Congressional Budget Office.

there is no law of nature that requires federal agencies to produce regulation in this way.

When it comes to the rule of law, that too can be reformed, especially with the right appointments to the Supreme Court. A new generation of justices could return the courts to the traditions of common law that used to inform judicial decision-making in this country.

Finally, we could improve education in this country simply by funding a lot of new and better schools. We have become trapped in a debate about public school education that simply omits the possibility that we could build better schools outside the public system.

Tocqueville was fundamentally an optimist about the United States. True, he feared that in the end the egalitarianism would get the better of liberty. There is an astonishing passage in *Democracy in America* where he imagines a future in which the central government becomes all-powerful. It is a nightmare vision of totalitarianism, of total individual dependence on government. However, on the whole, Tocqueville felt that such a fate was more likely to befall European democracies than to befall the United States. I share his belief that, at heart, Americans love their liberty too much to allow the exceptional institutions that safeguarded it for so long to be completely undermined.

One reason I moved from Harvard to the Hoover Institution is that this institution's core mission is to understand the institutions that preserve liberty, safeguard them, and strengthen them. I cannot think of any more important thing that a public intellectual could do in America today. And we are extremely fortunate that this institution exists, because it conspicuously has no counterpart in any other major university.

Notes

1. Anne Case and Angus Deaton, "Rising Morbidity and Mortality in Midlife among White Non-Hispanic Americans in the 21st Century," PNAS, September 17, 2015.

2. Charles Murray, *Coming Apart: The State of White America, 1960–2010* (New York: Crown Forum, 2012). See also J. D. Vance, *Hillbilly Elegy* (New York: Harper, 2016).

3. See, e.g., Raj Chetty, Nathaniel Hendren, Patrick Kline, Emmanuel Saez, and Nicholas Turner, "Is the United States Still a Land of Opportunity? Recent Trends in Intergenerational Mobility," NBER Working Paper No. 19844, www.nber.org /papers/w19844, (January 2014).

4. Niall Ferguson, *The Great Degeneration: How Institutions Decay and Economies Die* (London: Penguin, 2013).

5. Laurence J. Kotlikoff and Scott Burns, *The Clash of Generations: Saving Ourselves, Our Kids, and Our Economy* (Cambridge, MA: 2012).

8

What Makes America Great? Entrepreneurship

LEE OHANIAN

This chapter discusses the remarkable exceptionalism of American entrepreneurship and how entrepreneurship has been so critical in forging our nearly 250-year record of economic success. I will also discuss some policy options that can promote and foster entrepreneurship in the future.

America's vigorous entrepreneurial spirit predates the birth of our country by over a century and in fact goes back to 1607, which is the date of the first settlement in what became the thirteen colonies. One hundred and nine brave individuals from England set sail and came to the New World and settled in what is now known as Jamestown, Virginia. Contrary to popular belief, these settlers were not escaping religious persecution. Rather, this group represented 109 budding entrepreneurs. They were people who were undertaking the risk of a business and who came to Virginia with the idea that they were going to make a better life for themselves, with the hope of becoming successful.

Like most new businesses, the Virginia Company, which was the name of the Jamestown enterprise, failed miserably. The Virginia Company confronted the same challenges that any new business faces. These included difficulties in developing and implementing a business plan. In particular, the Virginia Company couldn't figure out which crops would flourish in Virginia. They also faced the more critical problems of trying to survive in environs so different from England.

As with many other new-business failures, the substantial risk of making a profit could not be overcome. But this failure also promoted future economic success. Subsequent settlers in Virginia learned from the miscues of the Virginia Company and found out through trial and error that tobacco would flourish in the Virginia climate. The demand for tobacco, and the rich soils of Virginia, made the new Virginians wealthy beyond their dreams. More broadly, the colonies grew from a few hundred settlers in the early 1600s to two million people—two million of the world's wealthiest people—just prior to the American Revolution. Entrepreneurship is part of America's DNA, and that same entrepreneurial spirit continues today.

To get a sense of the importance of entrepreneurship in the US economy, note that twenty-two American companies that began in 1976 or later are now among the five hundred largest corporations in the world, including Apple Computer, Microsoft, Google, and Costco. In contrast, continental Europe, which has a larger population than the United States, does not have a single company that began in 1976 or later among the largest five hundred in the world. Not surprisingly, it has enjoyed much less economic success over this period than the United States has.

Entrepreneurial continuity is critical for our future economic success, and entrepreneurs are the single most important force in driving economic growth and innovation. Just a few of our important entrepreneurs and their innovations and enterprises include Henry Ford and assembly-line production; the Wright brothers and the airplane; George Eastman and the camera; Bill Gates and Paul Allen of Microsoft; Steve Jobs of Apple Computer; Fred Smith of FedEx; Jeff Bezos of Amazon; and Howard Schultz of Starbucks.

These American entrepreneurs not only succeeded individually, but their success in turn created enormous wealth for society by way of creating new job and investment opportunities as well as new goods and services. In the process of developing and implementing their innovations, entrepreneurs transform the economy and the world that we live in. They are truly a gift to society. The wealth that they create for themselves is just a grain of sand on the beachfront that they create for the rest of us.

Today, the United States faces a crisis in entrepreneurship. The entrepreneurship rate, which is the number of new businesses started each year divided by the number of existing businesses, has declined by about 35 percent since the 1980s, and much of that decline has occurred since 2009.

To understand the importance of the current entrepreneurship deficit, I note that economic growth has change markedly in the United States since 2009. In particular, the United States is the only country that until recently enjoyed a largely uninterrupted and stable record of economic growth for over two hundred years. The historical average growth rate in per capita real gross domestic product, which is the most frequently used measure of a country's standard of living, is about 2 percent per year. This means that living standards in our country double about every thirty-five years.

However, America's remarkable record of stable economic growth is now in jeopardy. Figure 1 illustrates this problem by showing two lines.

The dashed line is the 2 percent growth trend described above. This line measures the expected position of our economy based on our historical record. The solid line shows actual per capita real GDP. The figure

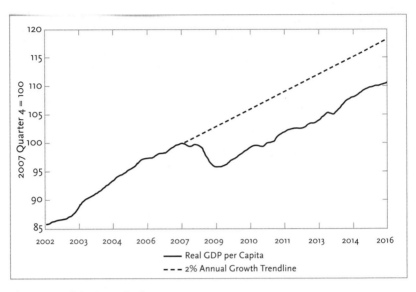

Figure 1. Real GDP per Capita

clearly shows the recession of 2008–9, and, more important, it shows that the economy has never recovered.

This is the first time in the history of the United States when the country did not recover from an economic downturn. To put this in perspective, the United States fully recovered from the Civil War and two world wars, from the Great Depression and the two major 1970s energy crises, from the savings and loan crisis, and from 12 percent inflation and nearly 20 percent interest rates of the early 1980s. But we haven't recovered from the 2008–9 recession, and this chart provides no evidence that we will. If the US economy had experienced a normal recovery after this recession, then the accumulated additional income over time, compared to our actual level of income, would nearly be enough to eliminate the US publicly held federal debt.

An important reason why we have not recovered is seen in the next graph (figure 2). I find this graph to be the most important and most depressing feature of our current economy, and it is one that you don't

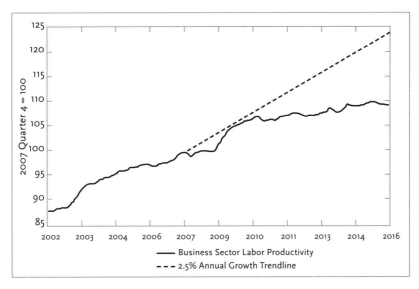

Figure 2. Productivity Is Well Below Trend

hear much about. It shows the enormous decline in the growth rate of worker productivity. American business sector productivity, which is the inflation-adjusted value added per worker, historically grew by about 2.5 percent per year. This means that it doubles every twenty-eight years. However, this growth rate has declined to about 0.9 percent per year. Consequently, you can see that there is now about a 14 percent gap between where our current productivity level is and where we should be. If productivity continues to grow at 0.9 percent per year, then it will double roughly every seventy-seven years, rather than its historical average of every twenty-eight years. This is a fundamental problem that we need to reverse to restore prosperity and growth.

Our current entrepreneurship deficiency has important implications for our current productivity-growth deficiency. To see this, note that all businesses have a life cycle. A few start-ups grow dramatically, become big, and transform the society that we live in. But ultimately, those businesses mature and then decline. A few big businesses, such as

IBM, which left computer hardware and is now in business consulting, and General Electric—which left consumer appliances and now specializes in medical imaging hardware and jet aircraft engines—reinvent themselves.

However, most big businesses are not able to reverse old age and succeed in other product lines. Does anybody remember Cone Mills or Hines Lumber or Pacific Vegetable Oil? They were all Fortune 500 companies and were an important part of our economic record at one time. But their decline is an equally important part of our economic record as new and better ideas come along and replace the old ideas.

The United States is not like continental Europe or South America, where large stagnant companies prosper because they receive subsidies and political payoffs. In contrast, the United States is a country that reallocates capital and labor from mature, declining businesses to very young growing businesses. In that process, the young replace the old within the life cycle of private enterprise. At one time, J. C. Penney, Woolworth, Montgomery Ward, and Sears ruled the American retail landscape. They have been pushed aside by Costco, Walmart, and Target.

Just before the financial crisis in 2006, start-ups created three and a half million jobs, while all incumbent businesses lost one million jobs. This statistic gives you a sense of how important entrepreneurs are for our economy.

In my view, our historically successful entrepreneurship record reflects four factors: an efficient financial system that has allocated capital to start-ups; historically sensible regulations; an excellent education system, which provided a deep pool of talented workers; and a tax code that didn't penalize small businesses.

More broadly, all of these factors historically reflect the United States' deep tradition of economic freedom. But all measures of our economic freedom have declined substantially. Before the financial crisis, the United States was ranked third in the world in terms of economic freedom, just behind Singapore and Hong Kong. Today we have fallen to sixteenth place, just behind Estonia.

This decline in economic freedom has coincided with a substantial increase in regulation, including financial regulation, a much lower ranked education system, and an increasingly complicated tax code that penalizes small business. Not surprisingly, this is the first time in the history of the United States that we have more exiting businesses than new businesses being born.

The United States substantially reduced regulatory burdens in the 1970s, 1980s, and 1990s, and this occurred under Republican and Democratic leaders. But since then, regulation has skyrocketed. The Small Business Administration commissioned a study to measure the cost of regulation. They estimated regulatory costs of $1.75 trillion in 2008, which had doubled from 2001. After 2008, these costs almost certainly have increased, with the Dodd-Frank Act and Obamacare. More broadly, Congress has chosen to delegate enormous regulatory authority to unelected commissions with no accountability whatsoever. These regulations cause disproportional impact on small business, including small banks. Lending to small business today is 20 percent below what it was during the financial crisis. How could that have happened?

A key problem is that the regulatory costs of the Dodd-Frank Act have increased the cost of lending, particularly to small community banks that do so much of the small-business funding in this country. Community banks are disappearing through consolidation, which is negatively impacting the financial system's capacity to make small-business loans.

The decline in the American education system is also negatively affecting entrepreneurs, who frequently report that it is hard to find qualified workers. Not so long ago, the American K–12 education system was the best in the world. Today, the Organisation for Economic Co-operation and Development, which administers international assessment tests in math and science to students, ranks us number twenty-seven out of thirty-four countries in international mathematical assessment. Our scores are comparable to, or even lower than, developing countries that spend 50 percent less per pupil. Why aren't our students performing better? In my view, teacher unions that protect underperforming teachers with teacher tenure are an important factor in this decline. The teacher dismissal rate for cause in California is just 0.003 percent. This means that only 3 out of every 100,000 teachers are dismissed for cause.

The dismissal rate for cause among workers in the private economy, however, is about 2,500 times higher. This suggests that teacher unions are protecting many poorly performing teachers through teacher-tenure provisions. Research by Hoover fellow Rick Hanushek shows that protecting underperforming teachers has an enormous negative effect on student learning. In particular, he finds that if the bottom tenth percentile of public school K–12 teachers were replaced with a median performing teacher, then US school achievement would rise from its current position near the bottom of the rankings to near the top.

Teacher unions not only keep poorly performing teachers in the classroom, but they also reduce the number of better performing teachers by blocking merit-based pay, which means that exceptional teachers are not paid what they are worth. In contrast, teacher union contracts typically link pay to tenure and training program certifications that are largely uncorrelated with teacher performance.

This discussion suggests that reforming teacher union contracts, particularly teacher tenure rules, and developing merit-based pay could have substantial positive effects on K–12 educational performance.

I now turn to what I call the dangerous "war on success" and how that's impacting entrepreneurship. Witness phenomena ranging from populist statements by former president Obama and Senator Elizabeth Warren, who have dismissed the importance of entrepreneurs, to policy proposals by former presidential candidates Hillary Clinton and Bernie Sanders, who have proposed raising tax rates substantially on the most productive earners. These increases include an investment surtax, a minimum tax rate that is referred to as the "Buffett Rule," much higher tax rates on capital gains, and a higher estate tax.

While these federal proposals will not become law under the current administration and the current Congress, there are similar proposals being made at the state and local government levels. This includes California's Proposition 55, which was passed in November. This proposition continues the 13.3 percent tax rate on the highest earners to 2030. This is particularly egregious because the 13.3 percent tax was explicitly marketed to voters by Governor Jerry Brown as a temporary tax to help restore California's fiscal stability following the recession. Voters approved the proposition with the view that "the rich can afford to pay, and the state needs the money."

A key to the passage of Proposition 55 was a populist strategy of allowing the higher state sales tax rate that was part of the original tax increase, and which impacted all Californians, to sunset. Not surprisingly, the proposition passed with over 63 percent of voters choosing to penalize the most productive workers in the state. Moreover, this clearly indicates that politicians will blatantly break promises if it means increasing revenue. Of course, this strategy, both with regard to breaking promises and with continuing to penalize success, may ultimately backfire if more high-earning Californians choose to leave the state. A study conducted by Spectrum Location Solutions, a firm that helps businesses determine where to locate, estimates that more than 10,000 businesses either left the state, substantially reduced operations, or chose not to locate in California between 2008 and 2015.

The war on success also takes place in the regulatory arena, particularly through the Dodd-Frank Act. The consumer protection bureau of the Dodd-Frank Act has been given almost an unconstrained ability to prosecute lenders. It has, for instance, prosecuted auto lenders for discrimination against minorities without any direct evidence of discrimination.

The consumer protection bureau guesses whether an individual is a minority based on their last name and address. Given such skimpy proof of discrimination, it is reasonable to wonder why a defendant would not fight this vigorously. It turns out, based on consumer protection bureau records, that the defendants in this lawsuit were chosen based on the expectation they would simply settle the suit. Is this consumer protection, which of course is the purpose of regulation, or is this a political shakedown of deep-pocketed lenders? It seems to me that this is a violation of our rule of law.

There has also been a substantial increase in regulatory intrusion in housing, including what are known as disparate impact lawsuits against business practices that are not discriminatory in terms of treating people differently but unintentionally harm a protected group. Typically, plaintiffs don't need to show that the practices intended to be discriminatory; they just need to show that the practice created a different outcome for a protected group.

Recently, a nonprofit organization promoting neighborhood integration sued the Texas Department of Housing for providing tax credits for new housing construction in minority neighborhoods. New investment within a neighborhood sounds like a welcome development, but not to the plaintiffs. Their logic is that new housing in a minority neighborhood improves the neighborhood, which in turn suggests that more families will remain in the neighborhood rather than move to other neighborhoods.

The lawsuit, and the pretzel logic defining the government's position, went to the Supreme Court in 2013. The plaintiff's case was argued by the US solicitor general, who adopted the view that improving minority neighborhoods interferes with the goal of integration. In questioning the solicitor general, Chief Justice John Roberts asked, "What is the bad thing, to build new housing in a minority neighborhood, or to build housing in an affluent neighborhood with the goal of increasing integration?" The solicitor general had no reasonable alternative but to agree with Roberts that both proposals would be regarded as positive developments for minorities. But despite Roberts's ridicule of the disparate-impact theory, the Supreme Court decided in favor, five to four, of the plaintiffs.

The examples described here show how policies have evolved over time to sharply restrict economic and personal freedom. Restoring prosperity requires restoring economic freedom, which in turn will promote entrepreneurship. Following the November 2016 elections, the country has a terrific opportunity to make policy changes in the areas of regulation, taxation, and education that could substantially improve the climate for entrepreneurs.

PART THREE

American Exceptionalism on the World Stage

9

American Dominance of the International Order

KORI SCHAKE

A hegemon is the state that sets and enforces the rules of the international order. In 1945, with the rest of the world in tatters, the United States had a dominant position, could have imposed its will on any other state. In characteristic American fashion, we had a raucous domestic debate—not about how to dominate the world but about whether to remain engaged in the world at all. Fortunately for our freedom and prosperity, American governments of both political parties chose, instead of isolation, to build an international order of rules, alliances, and institutions that invited and rewarded participation by other states on our terms. No other state victorious in war had ever attempted to share so widely the spoils of conquest. No other state had ever bought so cheaply such a long expanse of peace between great powers and economic growth shared so widely among states.

This achievement alone would mark the United States as unique in the history of the state system. We are a superpower that used the time of our dominance to create a system that was not reliant solely on our power to perpetuate itself. Historically, when a state becomes powerful, other states organize to confront it, to balance its power. Because the United States legitimated its power for other countries by participating in institutions and allowing itself to be constrained by the same rules that bound others, it has not engendered the same magnitude of opposition. As a result, the American order has been much less costly to maintain. We mostly don't have to enforce the rules.

Of course, it matters that we *can* enforce the rules. Our military strength and political willingness to fight wars about maintaining the order are essential. But because most states benefit from the rules we have established, we seldom have to impose them by force. The behavior that has historically driven the cycle of hegemonic rise and fall is the dominant power overextending itself and then being challenged by potential usurpers. By making American dominance about rules and institutions, our power has been less threatening to other states. Rather than seeking balance by opposing us, most states in the international order—and, crucially, the most powerful and prosperous states—see their interests as being served when they play by the same rules and participate in the same institutions as we do. America's challengers have tended to be states that cannot succeed by the rules we have established.

So the genius of the American order is that it is largely self-reinforcing. And no other state has proposed a model attractive enough to engender voluntary participation. The American system believes it is impossible for a state to have enduring economic prosperity without political liberty. The American system also is built upon the belief that the domestic political behavior of a state is a reliable indicator of its international behavior. Governments that allow themselves to be limited by law and are responsive to the will of their people are less likely to be threats to the American order. So we have fostered the creation and sustainment of other democratic governments, states that have the peaceful means to replace a government they no longer support.

This assortment of beliefs has been a radical departure from the norms of unlimited state sovereignty and policies that benefit the dominant state's power at the expense of others. America in its time of dominance has used its power not only for our own safety and enrichment but also for making possible those same things for others. We offer security that facilitates prosperity. We establish alliances to pool our strength and protect each other. We conclude trade agreements that foster more economic activity among rules-respecting states. We play by the rules and ensure others do as well. As a result, the American order rewards compliance, and the states that do comply become more like us over time and are therefore less likely to violently overthrow the order. The genius of this design has made American dominance enduring, even as other countries grow stronger, richer, and more involved in the international order. America's advantages are amplified in this international order.

Secretary of Defense Jim Mattis is fond of saying that the United States has two powers: the power of intimidation and the power of inspiration. If we look at the net favorability of attitudes toward the United States in various countries in the world, two facts are striking. The first is how large the group is of countries with citizenships that have very positive views of the United States. Notably, 89 percent of Iranians have a positive view. What this tells us is either that American policies are always smart, always positive, always beneficial (which is, of course, not true) or that citizens of certain countries give us credit even when they don't like our policies. It's a very common experience when one is abroad to hear, "Well, I don't like the American government, but I really like Americans," or "I don't like American policy on this, but I really like America." That's soft power at work. Our favorability is partly the result of our policies, but it's more than that. It's actually who we are as a political culture. It's about the truths we hold to be self-evident and how widely appealing they are to the aspirations of other people in the world.

Other countries want the success that the United States enjoys, even if they don't want the social and political consequences and wild cacophony of a system open enough that anybody can run for president and win. Other nations want to figure out how to have research universities like ours, the innovation of Silicon Valley, the financial esprit of Wall Street, and a blockbuster movie industry like Hollywood. Authoritarian countries try to create such outcomes without the messy, tumultuous freedom that makes them possible in the United States.

Nobody's done it yet. In the early 1990s, the political scientist Francis Fukuyama wrote a book called *The End of History and the Last Man,* which is now much derided. Of course, history hasn't ended, but his argument is a serious one, and it actually hasn't been disproven. He argues that freedom and prosperity are inherently linked and that there is no successful alternative to the American model. There may be challengers to it, but nobody has proven that you can actually be prosperous and stable over long periods of time without advocating the American model. Is there a country that is prosperous and lies outside of the American order, that doesn't have the rule of law, that doesn't have free expression? Is there a wealthy, stable society that doesn't play by the rules that we play by?

China is, of course, the most interesting test case. It became a rising power only when it began adopting the economic rules of the American order of free trade and free markets. It has not wholly adopted these rules: the government remains the major player in business, and the rule of law has not been reliably established. Yet enough opportunity was created to lift hundreds of millions of people out of poverty.

But can China keep a country without freedom, without the truths we hold to be self-evident, and still achieve political stability and prosperity? For the past forty years, China's government has instituted a set of policies that academics call authoritarian capitalism. It goes something like this: if the government helps you get rich, you have to accept that you won't have free speech, freedom of association, or freedom of religion. So far, it's working, but this is a crude measure of power in the international order because, of course, we seldom know that a system has stopped being effective until the government falls. The American model considers prosperity and repression incompatible—especially as a country moves up the economic value chain from extractive industry and manufacturing to a service economy and creative industries.

Whether China's leadership can maintain its repression and still become a genuine competitor of the United States for control of the international order is the central question of war and peace in our time. If it can, other states will migrate toward the Chinese model. Because what ruler wouldn't prefer not to have the annoyances of a free media and accountability to demanding constituents, to reward political allies with the most profitable opportunities?

And China definitely has a different model of international order in mind. The "Chinese dream" outlined by President Xi envisions China powerful and prosperous without the political liberalism that has characterized the American order. He is banking on the Chinese people being willing to accept prosperity without demanding political liberty.

Singapore is an interesting example. It is a minuscule country, unlikely to be scalable in its model, but it's an important outlier, and it will be fascinating to see whether it proves stable once the founding generation of Singapore passes from the scene—that is, whether people who are not associated with the creation of independence in Singapore can actually have the same hold over public attitudes. Will they have the same level of confidence from the public such that they don't need to have the kinds of broader representation in order to keep legitimacy?

If China, Singapore, and other variants on the authoritarian capitalism model prove that countries don't have to play by America's rules in order to get the good outcomes that the United States has, then we will be like Athens or Camelot: a moment of beauty in history that gets crushed by alternatives. Historians will ask why we squandered these enormous advantages that we had at the end of the twentieth century and the start of the twenty-first. We'll be a curiosity, like the collapsed Mayan civilization. "How did this happen?" they will ask. If the United States fails—that is, if the dominance that we have experienced in all of our lifetimes comes to an end—it will much more likely be the result of our own indiscipline than the assertive action of an adversary. As Abraham Lincoln said in a much more troubling time for our precious country, "If destruction is to be our lot we must ourselves be the authors of it."

Historically, hegemons reshape the order in their image. The strongest power, once it is powerful, starts to think about international relations the way its leaders think about their country's domestic relations. If one were to graph country wealth from 1500 forward, the lines would spike to represent the glory days of the Dutch Golden Age, the British Empire at its height in the nineteenth century, and the United States in the twentieth century. The only peaceful transition in the history of the state system was between Britain's hegemony and that of the United States. Every other such transition involved conquest. Why was this transition peaceful when no others have been peaceful?

There was friction between the United States and Britain in the nineteenth century. Just think about the War of 1812, when we defined our independence in contrast to what the British were. The British considered themselves a liberal government but not a democratic one. That is, they chose policies of open commerce; whereas the United States was, in the view of one British politician, "a country composed of elements so various and liable on all subjects to opinions so conflicting. They are a country of demagogues and non-entities."[1] It was only after a series of crises in the late nineteenth century that America and Britain began to look alike to each other—and to view themselves as a special pairing, distinct from every other country.

What transpired was that Britain had become a democracy, and the United States, because of the conquest of the American West, had come to be an empire. That is, we looked similar to each other and different from everybody else in the international order. Our power relative to each other mattered less than our cumulative power relative to other states. The British made a judgment that they could share responsibilities with us, trust us to handle the Pacific and let them handle the Mediterranean, because our interests were so much the same. Thucydides would be cheering. Fear, honor, and interests, he said, are what drive conflict. Our interests aligned as British fear and American honor came to be driving forces in our interactions.

Yet the British were wrong, as it turned out after a crucial twenty years, roughly from the late 1870s until the Spanish-American War. Once it had become the strongest power in the international order, the United States started trying to reshape that order in its own image. Rather than sustain an international order organized along British lines, we started chipping away at the legitimacy of the British Empire by arguing, for example, in the Versailles peace treaty after World War I, that all peoples are entitled to self-determination. We started to favor and to try to institute democratic governments, which Britain had not done. We started to try to create the international order in our image, and we have largely succeeded.

As the international order changes, it becomes more American. In the 2016 presidential political cycle, we had a big conversation about really basic questions—about America's role in the world. One issue was the complaint that our allies are not doing their fair share. It's true they are taking advantage of us. It would be nice if we could trade them in for better allies, but there are no better allies to be had. We have the best ones in the international order already.

For all of the burdens we bear for our allies, fewer Americans die in our wars because of them. Playing team sports means sharing the burdens of what we are trying to achieve in the world. Our allies are our regional intelligence networks. They're our diplomatic partners, who feed ideas into our policy making. They offer their markets, their territory, their treasury, and their soldiers to our common causes. And it is our ability to draw people in on our side that is the genius of the American order. It is what actually makes it possible for us to achieve as much as we do, and it's harder and more expensive without them, as tiresome as they are.

I was the poor taxpayer who had to work coalition politics during the Iraq War, from 2003 to 2005. So I know it's tiresome dealing with recalcitrant allies, but it is actually so much better than the alternatives. Our trade agreements cement our political agreements and build linkages that make us all richer. The institutions that we so often complain about—the United Nations, the North Atlantic Treaty Organization, the World Trade Organization—are not only American creations. They are burden-sharing devices that make possible everything that we're trying to do. They are the secret to American dominance.

Some ask, can't America leave the world's troubles to someone else to manage? The way to think about the problem of international order without American dominance is by asking: What would this world be like if we were not the people setting the rules? Vacuums get filled. And they get filled very often by states and people whose rules we would not like. We would not like a Chinese tribute system, where prosperity is by sufferance of the government. We would not like a Russian mafia state. We would not like the incapacity of a European-dominated world. We would not like the prosperity-sapping entropy that disorder would bring to our society.

We've suffered in the past from the form of insecurity we're now experiencing about our country's future. In the 1950s we had a strikingly similar conversation about Germany and the *Wirtschaftswunder,* the great advance of German industry. With Japan in the 1980s, we saw that they were good at manufacturing in a way that we just weren't. Now it's China. But perhaps it's Singapore we should be trying to emulate in some (though not all) ways. Theirs is a much more successful and sustainable model than China's.

The kind of manufacturing that has made China prosperous resembles that of America in the nineteenth century. Theirs are probably not jobs we want now. The jobs we want are innovation driven. And the government we want certainly isn't China's. The Chinese government has many executive advantages that ours does not. In a disgraceful *New York Times* column, Thomas Friedman wrote that he wished the American government could be like China's, where it didn't respect the rights of its citizens so it could build railroads that run at high speeds.[2] Some believe China is great and we're inefficient, but very few Americans want to trade away the things that make it difficult to get consensus on high-speed railroads in this country.

It's tempting, though, to think that China is making enormous advances and we can't counter them. Russia, too, is making interesting and important strategic choices that have moved it into the vacuum that we left during the Obama administration.

The Obama doctrine, laid out in the erstwhile president's extraordinary interviews with Jeffrey Goldberg of the *Atlantic,* backslid away from the assertive changing of the international order. He had more faith in institutions without us driving those institutions as we traditionally have. He had more faith in leading from behind than leading from the front. The problem with leading from behind is that it requires allies to follow from the front, and most allies won't do that. Many allies can't.

One example of America leading from behind, and doing it right, occurred during the Clinton administration, right after the debacle in Somalia. East Timor was breaking away from Indonesia. The United States very much wanted this to happen peacefully, but there was no way we could contribute to the United Nations force after Somalia. The Australian government of John Howard was actually willing to, and the US government quietly offered the Australians any help they needed to succeed. We gave them a blank check. They stepped forward and did an outstanding job, and because they succeeded in that, they gained the confidence to take a much more active international role, as we have seen in Iraq and Afghanistan, and in everything we have tried to do since then.

Contrast that to President Obama's approach in Libya, where we stepped back and expected allies to do most of the work, and yet we still took much of the credit for it. The NATO ambassador and the NATO military commander, both Americans, outlined in the *New York Times* all the ways in which American forces were "critical and irreplaceable," leaving allies disgruntled.[3] That's how you get allies to hang back and not do anything. We need to actually get good at encouraging allies again.

We shouldn't lose hope. Look at the 2016 Freedom House annual survey of freedom in the world. In 1985, the world was roughly split between free states and unfree states, with some partially free. The United States usually tops the league tables of free states. Unfree states are obvious. Partially free states are those, like Singapore, where there is the rule of law but the government is not accountable in the same way that Western governments are. What you see over time is that the number of free states is increasing. The big increase after the end of the Cold War peaked in 2005, and we have since been seeing some erosion in the international order. But we are also seeing a line that, even if it jags like a stock market daily report, is nonetheless going up over the long term.

Today, our biggest challenges, the challenges to our dominance, are all predominantly domestic. To cite Theodore Roosevelt's 1904 annual message to Congress, "The eternal vigilance which is the price of liberty must be exercised sometimes to guard against outside foes, although of course far more often to guard against our own selfish or thoughtless shortcomings."[4] The worst of these selfish and thoughtless shortcomings is the fact that we are spending our children's inheritance at a time when we aren't even facing great and enormous challenges. The debt is the biggest national security risk the United States is running, and we are doing it voluntarily. We ought to be very worried about that.

We need to defang the fear of change—the economic and social change that people had such strong reactions to in the recent election cycle. People are worried by the pace and magnitude of change. This would all be easier to handle if our economy were growing faster. The rebuilding of consensus about the need to stop spending money we don't have would be the best thing we could do to strengthen America's role in the world.

To return to Jim Mattis's point about the powers of intimidation and inspiration: one reason that we are such an inspiring model to the world is that we have tended to govern ourselves well. But in 2028 our debt will reach the 100 percent mark of GDP. By 2039, based on current projections, it will be nearly double that. The affordability of our debt will be drastically reduced when interest rates start going back up. We need to solve this problem while it is still manageable. We are on an unsustainable path that is absolutely of our own making. The ability of the United States to rejuvenate itself has been a great source of strength and a surprise to adversaries for generations, but this is arithmetic.

Yet for all of the things that we do badly right now, we very often underestimate the things other states would have to do well to overtake the United States. That is so even if we believe that the rules the United States has established—the rule of law, free markets, free trade—are unnecessary and that a rising China can remain authoritarian and still surpass the United States to become the rule setter of the international order. There are a lot of things we do well that we don't actually give ourselves much credit for.

Russia is a danger to us through its failure, not through its success. The Chinese have yet to navigate the middle-income trap, to advance beyond extractive industries and basic manufacturing. They're getting there, but they're not there yet. They have yet to make the transition from an economy of exports to one of domestic consumption, to grapple with an aging population and a society that's intolerant of immigration. President Xi's crackdown on dissent suggests that they are deeply concerned that ideas of freedom are gaining traction in the Chinese population. This explains the great firewall they have erected to block the Internet: they are genuinely afraid they may not continue holding on to power. The extensive anti-corruption campaign that Xi is overseeing does not appear to be outrunning corruption because he's not running out of people to prosecute.

Then there is the costliness of primacy should China gain it. The advantage of the US system is that, because the order is largely voluntary, it is much less expensive to enforce. Countries choose to create forms of government similar to ours; to accept the rule of law; to accept tolerance—we don't make them. The greater the extent to which they do so, the greater the share of prosperity that accrues to them. The genius of the American order is that good things go together. What we tend to see is economic and political outcomes in which stability is coupled with economic prosperity. The rules that China seems intent on setting benefit no country other than China. As a result, they will have to use much more coercion to enforce their order than we do. Consider the South China Sea, where the United States was trying to get all of the countries in the region to cooperate in pushing back with a united front against China's assertive, unilateral building of new islands for military airstrips.

But it's never easy. The new president of the Philippines was making offensive statements about President Obama and threatening to throw the United States out of the Philippines. Our government very wisely did what Lyndon Johnson did when the French behaved similarly in 1965, which is to calmly say, "When a man asks you to leave his house, you take your hat and go."[5] What the Philippines is likely to find is that the United States may be a problematic ally, but they, too, have few better choices than opting in to the American-led order. So it is for nearly every other country.

If we fix our own problems and we remind ourselves that allies are worth having—that an order constructed across these seventy years is actually principally in our interests, not just in other peoples' interests—and we remind ourselves that we're actually good at a lot of things that other countries struggle to get right, then I bet our grandchildren's grandchildren will still be living in a world of American dominance.

Notes

1. Quoted in Paul Crook, "Whiggery and America: Accommodating the Radical Threat," in *Radicalism and Revolution in Britain, 1775–1848: Essays in Honour of Malcolm I. Thomis,* ed. Michael T. Davis (London: Palgrave-Macmillan, 2000), 198.

2. Thomas L. Friedman, "Our One-Party Democracy," *New York Times,* September 8, 2009, www.nytimes.com/2009/09/09/opinion/09friedman.html (accessed May 18, 2017).

3. Ivo H. Daalder and James G. Stavrides, "NATO's Success in Libya," *New York Times,* October 31, 2011.

4. Theodore Roosevelt, "Fourth Annual Message," December 6, 1904, The American Presidency Project, www.presidency.ucsb.edu/ws/?pid=29545 (accessed May 19, 2017).

5. Lyndon Johnson quoted in Thomas Alan Schwartz, *Lyndon Johnson and Europe: In the Shadow of Vietnam* (Cambridge, MA: Harvard University Press, 2003), 105.

The Foundations of America's Exceptional Role in the World

VICTOR DAVIS HANSON

"Exceptionalism" doesn't necessarily mean "preeminence." It's derived from a Latin word *excipere*—"to take from" or "to select" or "to differentiate." The English concept is the same as in Latin: to take out something from the majority or take it away from the implied normal group. In theory an "exceptional" trait could be bad or good. But in the context of the United States, we mean that America is positively weird. It's fortunately odd. It's thankfully different. In other words, America is not like most nations but preferable to them.

There are numerous transcendent building blocks of civilization that, throughout history, predict whether a particular society will prove dynamic or ossified. One is demography. Does a society's popu-

---

The above text is an edited transcript of an orally delivered lecture.

lation grow, or is it static or even shrinking? Let's look at comparisons with the Western or Westernized industrial world today. Until very recently we grew at a little over 1 percent annual growth rate. In recent years, the United States has seen slower population growth apart from immigration, but still, compared to our fellow Western or Westernized industrialized nations (for example, Germany at 0.5 percent, Japan at −0.01 percent, or Italy at 0.0 percent), we are a young nation. Robust demography in some sense is based on confidence in a society's future, or perhaps assumes some sense of transcendence; in classical terms, the elderly plant an olive tree that will not produce fruit in their lifetime on the assumption that subsequent generations will enjoy the orchard's harvests. Generational confidence and continuity—as well as a robust younger population—hinge on fertility.

The United States is a more religious country than most of its Western counterparts. Americans still believe in transcendence, or something divine beyond our corporeal existence, and that fact can manifest itself in greater fertility as well and in confidence that family raising is part of the human experience and the perpetuation of the species. Again, the pragmatic Greeks reminded generations that parents change their babies' diapers so that one day their children can change theirs. Obviously, the recent assumption of that role of caring for the elderly by socialist and welfare states helps obviate the need for child-rearing and, indirectly—along with agnosticism, greater affluence, and urbanization—discourages fertility.

Racial and ethnic diversity, if accompanied by assimilation, integration, and intermarriage, rather than tribalism, can fuel national strength and widen appeals to immigrants. Currently, it is popular to talk and brag about our diversity. Yet it is a bit more complicated than that. Throughout history, diversity, in fact, has been a great bane of civilizations. It has been a disadvantage, often resulting in sectarianism and tribal violence. In contrast, almost mono-racial Japan and China are powerful countries that prize uniformity, sameness, and order. They're not all that diverse. Diversity through the ages was a challenge to be overcome, not an innate advantage to be automatically enjoyed. Yet the United States is the only major country that is a truly stable multiracial and democratic society—a melting pot different from both tribal and violent Iraq, Rwanda, and the former states of Yugoslavia—and also different from their more stable mono-racial antitheses that conflate race with citizenship and are virtually unable to absorb diverse immigrants. Assimilating diverse groups into a national body politic divorces race from nationalism and in theory should make diverse immigration a positive meritocratic experience.

Another reflection of civilizational dynamism is the stuff of life: food and fuel, specifically agriculture and fossil-fuel production. Take the latter. Remember that just thirty years ago experts warned that the United States had reached the era of "peak oil" and that by the early twenty-first century there would be less oil left in the ground than had already been exploited, leaving the United States vulnerable to foreign pressures to ensure the importation of 70 percent of our needed oil and natural gas. Yet the United States proved to be the only major nation that could flip "peak oil" on its head and become self-sufficient in fossil fuels—not just because it sits on naturally endowed soil, but also because it is one of the exceptional nations in the West that ensures private property and mineral rights and the ability to verify such claims and titles, and to easily transfer ownership of them. In addition, America also exceptionally encourages private-sector innovation in a way that unfortunately Europe does not. The ability to produce fuels and electrical energy cheaply and plentifully translates into a more efficient transportation system and industrial base—and thus greater competitiveness among Western exporters.

A few years ago, in the *Wall Street Journal,* an article warned that twenty-first-century America might well become a net food importer—as population increased and domestic agriculture reached peak production. Yet we're not a net food importer today. The United States is still exporting food worldwide, from beef to rice to perishable produce to dried fruit. Somehow the private farming sector in the United States has been able to squeeze out additional production per acre, which had seemed previously to be finite—largely because of a traditional belief in farming as a private enterprise as well as a symbiosis between agriculture and advanced technology and applied research in private and public universities.

Higher education—along with population growth, ethnic and racial stability, and efficient fuel and food production—is yet another index of civilizational strength. I mentioned on an earlier occasion that the (London) *Times Higher Education*'s World University Rankings—a foreign, not domestic, arbiter of university excellence—in its annual comparisons of the universities in the world ranks American campuses the highest among its top five hundred educational institutions. Indeed, California alone usually places four to five universities (California Institute of Technology, Stanford University, University of California–Berkeley, University of California–Los Angeles, and sometimes University of Southern California) among the top twenty—more so than almost all other countries except the United States as a whole—largely as a result of excellence in such areas as business, medicine, computer science, and engineering. In sum, the United States is not just exceptional in terms of its higher education system, it is preeminent—a fact, of course, that offers America enormous additional economic and military advantages.

In terms of relative economic power, even today in America's so-called decline, its 320 million people produce almost twice as many goods and services per annum as does China's 1.3 billion, the next largest economy other than the combined nations of the European Union. In crude and inexact terms, essentially one American is producing almost twice as many goods and services as do four Chinese today. This advantage is not just because of years of a technological head start, but rather is also due to the rule of law, consensual government, and a tradition of free labor and capital working more or less in concert under transparent free enterprise.

In terms of military dynamism, the American military is a reflection of these advantages in fuel, food, demography, diversity, constitutional stability, and economic growth. America's military preeminence in turn naturally translates into greater political reach and influence in the world. An exceptional country like the United States can spend more on defense than the next dozen countries in aggregate and yet still keep its military expenditures below 4 percent per annum because of its innately robust economy and political cohesion.

When the United States didn't field a preeminent military, as was true in 1914 and 1939, it nonetheless had the ability to do so—and in relatively short order. Take the example of World War I when Americans initially sat out the conflict. We did not want any part of Europe's entangling alliances and wars, perhaps heeding the warnings of the Founders. Yet quite suddenly in April 1917, Woodrow Wilson took an unarmed United States to war. The American military of the time was little more than a frontier constabulary force that had fossilized in the West since the nineteenth century. Yet between April 1917 and November 1918, a mere twenty months, the US military created a new expeditionary force of two million soldiers and was able to transport them to the shores of France without losing a soldier in transit to enemy operations. The very idea that the Imperial German Army—the greatest field army in the history of military conflict up to 1914—could have transported two million German soldiers and landed them on the East Coast of the United States is absolutely absurd. Only the United States had the logistical and lift capacity to project such force, largely because of its exceptional economic power, technology, and political stability.

The United States also entered World War I with no munitions industries to speak of. Yet in twenty months Americans were producing more artillery shells than were France and Britain, who had been refining their arms industry for four years. This exact sort of transformation again happened in 1939. Americans had initially sworn they would stay out of yet another European conflict. Indeed, the United States had an army smaller than Portugal's in 1939 and was ranked somewhere near twentieth worldwide in relative budgetary percentages of military expenditures. Although the United States came late into the war against all three Axis powers, in a mere four years the military had grown to over 12 million soldiers. America only had a population of around 130 million people in 1940; in comparison, the Soviet Union had 170 million. Its Red Army was the largest military in the history of warfare at 12.5 million in uniform. Yet as a country of 40 million fewer people, the United States fielded forces roughly the same size as the Soviet military, even though it was relatively disarmed in 1940.

In 1938–39 the United States was spending about 1 percent of its budget on defense. Fast forward: the annual GDP of the United States by 1945 was roughly the same as the combined productive output of its enemies Japan and Germany, as well as those of its allies Britain and Russia. Of some 600,000 airframes that were produced in World War II, the United States built 400,000. America produced 90 percent of the aviation fuel in World War II. I could go on, but you see the point: when these unique attributes—food, fuel, education, demography, relative social harmony, free-market economics—were combined under a politically stable system, then the logical result was a dynamic military and an exceptional military-industrial base.

During the Cold War the existential challenge was how to stop five hundred divisions of the Soviet Union from overrunning Western Europe and from expanding into the Korean Peninsula, Japan, and southeast Asia. By the time of the Korean War (June 1950), despite the dismantling of the American World War II military, US forces were able to stop communist armies from absorbing Korea south of the 38th parallel. Rarely in history has one country stepped forward to sponsor an economic, political, and cultural global framework that would allow even its former enemies, such as Germany and Japan, to excel under rules of trade and commerce that it had sanctioned and enforced with a superior military that had sought no conquest or territory.

The United States has not annexed anyone's territory through conquest since doing so in the Philippines in 1898. I'm named after a Victor Hanson who was killed while serving with the Sixth Marine Division on Okinawa on Sugar Loaf Hill on May 19, 1945. I was reading his letters not long ago, and he wrote about not wishing to be deployed so far from home but was nonetheless proud to join the marines in the expulsion of the Japanese from their Greater East Asia Co-prosperity Sphere in the Pacific. Yet after the United States took Okinawa from the Japanese, it eventually gave the island back to them. Few other countries in history can forget the wounds of war to show such magnanimity. When Russia invaded many of the Sakhalin Islands (taken against minimal opposition), it kept them and is still undergoing a dispute with Japan. In sum, at great cost, the United States helped Western democracies win two world wars and implode the Soviet communist empire during the Cold War, lost a great deal of blood and treasure, and yet did not turn its military successes into territorial or imperial acquisitions.

This is not to say that there were not tragic miscalculations and setbacks, from Vietnam to Iraq. But if we are currently remorseful about the controversial Iraq War, it nevertheless fits the general pattern of US interventions. The United States removed a genocidal dictator. It did not annex Iraq's oil wealth but instead fostered a democratic government, which by 2011 was viable and fairly stable—at least until the United States abruptly pulled out. But to offer a comparison to the 2011 Iraq withdrawal: imagine if Dwight Eisenhower, up for reelection in 1956, for the price of a campaign talking point, had announced that he was pulling all troops out of South Korea on the premise that his administration had not started the US engagement there; that violence was relatively absent by 1956; and that the expense of occupation and peacekeeping was too costly. Had we done something in 1956 analogous to our 2011 pullout from Iraq, there would be no South Korea today, no

Samsung, no Kia, no South Korean democracy—but simply a macabre North Korean government occupying the entire Korean Peninsula.

In sum, the postwar system was a product of exceptional American economic, political, and military dynamism that cannot be explained by either the size of American territory or population. The effort was neither imperial nor neocolonial, and yet it was often critiqued as something akin to the hegemony of the Soviet Union or of the prior British or Ottoman empires. Perhaps this is a symptom in the West of how leisure and affluence often offer citizens the luxury of imagining that because they were not perfect in their behavior then they were not a force for good or that the sins of humankind—sexism, racism, class exploitation—are theirs alone. Often Americans are either unaware of, or reluctant to ponder, their exceptionalism, and the result is that other nations and cultures often sense such hesitancy, see it as a confession of national guilt and weakness to be exploited rather than of magnanimity to be appreciated, and then rechannel such criticism on the global stage. To be reductionist, if Americans do not appear to appreciate their unique culture, then why should they expect that others would?

Are America's advantages constant? Has American preeminence reached a sense of the end of history in which democratic market capitalism and Western notions of personal freedom guarantee perpetual preeminence?

Hardly. America's present adherence to unique values is not set in stone or predestined to remain constant. In that context, let us reexamine these civilizational building blocks that can lead to exceptional power overseas. Look again at American education. While still preeminent, American academia is starting to resemble the medieval university. If we were at the University of Padua, in 1500, and if we were to suggest—even though the Renaissance era had made enormous strides in technology and science—that the earth, in fact, revolved around the sun, rather than vice versa, we would find ourselves branded as heretics and face near lethal consequences.

In the same fashion, I would imagine if a young assistant professor of science at Stanford University were up for tenure and he wrote a paper suggesting that there was some evidence that the earth had not heated up in the prior seventeen years, or that if it had, such slight warming was neither man-caused nor posed an existential threat, or that even massive outlays in government expense would not do much to arrest slight warming, then he would be likely seen as heretical and not given tenure. In contrast, imagine a young scholar in the 1960s suggesting *H. pylori* rather than stress alone causes stomach ulcers: Would he be ostracized in the present fashion for questioning so-called settled science? I think there are areas in the university today that are starting to become very medieval. And if such self-imposed censorship and harassment of free inquiry continue, eventually it will creep into our business schools, the very teaching of science, and perhaps result in something like postmodern engineering. Any time one stifles free speech and open inquiry for whatever perceived noble reason, it will have an effect of thwarting humanism and undermining values of the Enlightenment, as it has in the past.

With regard to demography, I'm also a little worried; our fertility rates, while not at European levels, have dropped. As an aside, during the 2016 election cycle I had been reading the WikiLeaks trove and had noted especially what Hillary Clinton and her team said of Bernie Sanders's supporters: that they were just a bunch of guys who lived in their parents' basements and were suffering from prolonged adolescence. I must confess that in this case I almost agree with her team about such a profile of many millennials. Our replacement rate has gone from near 2 percent in recent years down to near 1 percent. The culprit may be economic stagnation or the pressure of popular culture or our changing sociology or politics; nonetheless, we have a new cohort of youth that is not confident in the old American paradigm of marrying early, raising children, purchasing a house, and settling into full-time employment. Our current social, political, economic, and cultural uncertainty also contributes to childlessness. In historical terms, there are significant repercussions resulting from stagnant demography: erosion in military readiness, decreased economic vitality, and the growth of an unsustainable social-welfare state.

Diversity has always been a challenge to societies rather than an innate advantage. Here, too, I'm very worried because not only are we dividing into blue states and red states ideologically—two coastal corridors of elites versus a sea of conservative red in between—but we are also a hyphenated population. We strive to find victim status and the careerist advantages of what that entails through emphasizing and sometimes exaggerating claims of aggrieved minority status. The idea of *e pluribus unum* is considered passé, along with that of the melting pot, as difference rather than assimilation is seen to offer an edge in employment and admissions. In the past, tribal sectarianism developed a life of its own and could eventually unwind a previously stable society. If that fragmentation should accelerate, then it is difficult to appeal to a common body politic, which in turn likewise erodes military readiness, political stability, and the basic security and safety of the average citizen. We are currently in a war between the formidable powers of intermarriage, integration, and assimilation and those of tribalism and separatism; it is not clear which force will prove the more powerful.

If we look at the status of fossil fuels, all our expertise and sophisticated petrology do not do much good if a society decides that it is not going to use a safe technology and take advantage of our traditions of definable property rights and of the can-do culture of American entrepreneurialism and optimism. In other words, if we can't complete the Keystone Pipeline System, or if, in the manner of Germany, we decide to spend massively to subsidize currently expensive wind and solar sources of power and neglect clean-burning natural gas for largely ideological rather than fact-based reasons of economic rationality, then there's no intrinsic reason why a resource-rich America would not go the way of

Europe and become once again a net importer of expensive energy—with all that entails for economic competitiveness.

The same complacency can affect our current advantages that accrue from a dynamic agriculture. I was driving recently across central California. The wind was up to about forty miles per hour at two o'clock in the afternoon on the "West Side" where irrigation deliveries have almost been ended largely due to political obstructionism and environmental lawsuits, leaving vast tracts of ground fallow. The dust reminded me of photos of the 1930s Dust Bowl. The reason for such chaos was that about a million acres had been taken out of production for want of contracted irrigation water. When elites either do not know of, or do not appreciate, the tragedy and the hardship inherent in agriculture—the age-old challenges of producing food—then they are prone to do inexplicable things, such as cutting off irrigation water to the most productive land on the planet on the theory that the three-inch smelt of the San Francisco Bay delta requires more oxygenated water in its habitat and such additional freshwater must come at the expense of diverting canal deliveries from formerly irrigated farmland. If that mind-set were to continue, there would be widespread repercussions. Societies decline not just due to a dearth of food and fuel but also due to a paralysis in their ability to develop such assets on hand.

If that complacency were to spread, it would be reminiscent of 1960, when I was a little boy and my parents said we're going to go out to the West Side of the San Joaquin Valley to shoot varmints. But we were first warned to wear handkerchiefs because the pre-agricultural wasteland out there was dry and dusty, and the spores of a potentially fatal Valley Fever were in the fall air. The alternative to cultivation is not paradise; the wild is not always innocuous. Our agricultural preeminence is dependent upon realizing the thin line between civilization and hunger. Agriculture is predicated on living one more day. One more day—that's all farming is: producing enough food ensures that we are not hunter-gatherers engaged in twenty-four-hour quests for food—as was the case for most of the history of man until 7,000 years ago. If we Americans reach a period when we think we deserve exemption from nature's laws and we can sustain 320 million people and take a million acres out of production here, a million acres there—because of theories about a bait fish being a barometer of the entire ecosystem—then all the agricultural expertise and years of technological advancement by these brilliant farmers would be rendered null and void, and we would return to the preindustrial plight of man, which is not pretty.

The look at the challenges facing our previously preeminent areas of education, food, fuel, diversity, and demography also suggests that they will eventually affect the US military. We all read different statistical tables and figures, but if we were to look at the spending percentages of the present-day military and then compute the share devoted to salaries, retirement, and health care, then we would find that the United States is spending anywhere from 25 percent to 30 percent of our total military budget in a way that the Chinese and the Russians are not. Such imbalances require a readjustment of military evaluation, given that our enemies free up more relative capital for weapons and training. That China or Russia may be much closer to our own level of technological acquisitions or investments in high-tech weaponry than we think is revealed by the relative size of their military budgets.

I have not spoken at length of our wonderful constitutional system of federalism, which ensures both unity and flexibility of governance at the state and local levels. But here again, we are facing unprecedented challenges to the very cohesion of the federal system. Take so-called sanctuary cities. If through executive orders or local legislation some three-hundred entities declare themselves sanctuary jurisdictions where federal immigration law does not apply, in theory we are returning to the nullification crises of the Jacksonian era or indeed to the disaster of 1860–61, which led to secession. In theory, if sanctuary cities prevail, there's nothing, for example, to stop a conservative city like Cody, Wyoming, from declaring that gun registration would not apply within its city limits.

I don't always appreciate the federal Endangered Species Act. But under the nullification theory of sanctuary cities, suppose, in the environs of Provo, Utah, local magistrates declare that Environmental Protection Agency (EPA) statutes do not apply. We could then see EPA sanctuary cities spread. Nullification of federal law, for whatever reason, unwinds a republic—and these constitutional fissures will likewise have ramifications in our military and foreign policy.

The present postwar and global order championed by the United States is not a preordained fact. It is again an oddity based on American exceptionalism. And American overseas leadership ultimately is based on the strange idea that a country today of only 320 million people could have such inordinate military power and diplomatic influence, due largely to its educational excellence, its energy resources, its dynamic agriculture, its political stability, and its demographic confidence.

If at home our vitality were to be eroded—that is, if we were to scale back our current approach to agriculture and energy, reformulate the university, recalibrate the constitutional glue that holds us together, become consumers rather than producers, cease being confident in the future and thus in raising families, then the United States would become simply unable to exercise global leadership, and we would outsource influence abroad to different regional hegemonies—Iran, Russia, China, radical Islam—and ultimately we and our democratic allies would be less safe here at home.

Russia seems intent on carving out a hegemony in the area that was once the former Soviet Union and perhaps even extending its spheres of influence to the area of the former Warsaw Pact. China sees the South China Sea as a *mare nostrum*. Iran envisions a Shiite caliphate for the Persian Gulf. ISIS slaughters for a radical Sunni empire in the Middle

East. North Korea is an unpredictable nuclear nihilist. The problem with all these regional agendas is that historically there's no evidence that any of these entities have ever acted out of disinterested influence, at least to the degree that the United States has been disinterested in its world leadership. Without traditions of consensual government, free-market capitalism, or human rights, their versions of hegemony are quite different from the influence the United States has exercised in Europe and Asia.

I'd like to conclude with a thought. I've mentioned material conditions that promote military preeminence and an exceptional role abroad. But spirit and collective confidence matter as well. Ascendance is in part psychological. Decline is not fated. Instead, withdrawal and recession are usually choices.

For example, when I review the Greek city-state (and I spent most of my life writing about the history of the *polis*), I see that its decline is somewhat mysterious. In 480 BC, the 1,500 or so Greek city-states were faced with an existential threat. They were relatively poor. Democracy at Athens was only twenty-six years old. A quarter-million Persians under King Xerxes were marching southward through Thessaly, accompanied by a huge fleet descending along the northern Greek coast to destroy the city-states. Yet impoverished and vastly outnumbered Hellenic troops stopped them for three days at Thermopylae; then, again, they defeated the Persian fleet a few weeks later at Salamis. And they finally defeated and essentially destroyed the Persian army at Plataea a year later.

Fast forward 150 years. In 338 BC, the city-states again faced threats approaching from the north. But unlike their ancestors, the Greek city-states now were far larger and more powerful. Their armies and navies were much more impressive than were those of their great-grandparents, and indeed their economies were richer and more balanced than was the monarchy of Philip II of Macedon, who threatened to absorb them.

We think now that Alexander and Phillip were always unstoppable military geniuses. Yet in 338 BC, when compared to the past militaries of the Persians, they were hardly great captains at the head of invincible armies. Philip II never put in the field more than thirty thousand men. Yet in 338 BC he defeated the Greek city-states at the Battle of Chaeronea, and within ten years the *polis* had ceased to exist as a free state.

A similar paradox occurred at Rome. Hannibal and his Carthaginian forces during the Second Punic War posed an existential threat to Italy. In a series of battles between 219 and 216 BC, a very poor, agrarian Italian republic lost perhaps a hundred thousand men—a quarter of the adult male population of the Roman Republic. And yet the Romans defeated Hannibal, and by 202 had landed in Africa to drive him out of his home at Carthage.

Again, fast forward, seven hundred years. Rome was not a mere one-quarter of the Italian Peninsula, as it had been in the third century BC, but encompassed seventy million people by the fifth century AD and perhaps one million square miles of territory. And yet its legions could not stop a series of existential threats from the north from what in the past would have been written off as the raids of backward tribes and thugs—Visigoths, Ostrogoths, Vandals, and Huns. By any historical measure, these northern tribes posed far less relative danger to a vast Roman Empire than did Hannibal to a poor agrarian Roman Republic.

What am I getting at through these historical references? Material strength is often predicated on collective spirit and confidence.

Why is the United States seemingly withdrawing from its world responsibilities? Why did the Greeks fight much less effectively when they were much richer? Why did the Romans have much less confidence when they were wealthier and more influential?

In part, different generational mentalities determine a civilization's confidence or lack of the same, which in turn calibrates its military strength and cultural power. Economic vitality can explain only so much. If one arises in the morning and believes that his country is no better than the alternative, or if one follows a mind-set that one must be perfect to be considered good, then history seems to suggest collective stasis, ossification, self-doubt, and paralysis have set in. Indeed, history is cruel to civilizations that spend rather than invest, that become diffident about their culture—and that see little distinction between themselves and the vastly different alternatives abroad.

PART FOUR

The Spirit of American Exceptionalism

Herbert Hoover and
American Exceptionalism

GEORGE H. NASH

During his very long life Herbert Hoover developed a political and social philosophy that he believed could explain the greatness of the country he loved. To understand his vision of American exceptionalism, we need to understand the exceptional shape of his career before he entered American public life.

Hoover was born in 1874 in the little Quaker community of West Branch, Iowa, a son of the village blacksmith. Before he was ten, both of his parents had died. From Iowa, in 1885, he was sent to live with the family of an uncle in Oregon, where he stayed for nearly six years. In 1891 he entered Stanford University as a member of its Pioneer Class. At Stanford he flourished, graduating in 1895 with a degree in geology and an ambition to become a mining engineer.

From then on, his rise in his chosen profession was rapid. In 1897 his San Francisco employer recommended him for a position in Western Australia with an eminent British firm of mining engineers. Hoover's journey from California to Australia via New York, London, France,

Italy, and the Suez Canal, was a tremendously stimulating experience for a young man of twenty-two. Years later he remarked significantly: "History became a reality and America a contrast."[1]

Upon arriving in Western Australia, Hoover headed for the gold-fields in the desolate outback, where he would live for the next year and a half. After one arduous trip far into the bush, he wrote to a cousin: "Am on my way back to Coolgardie. Am glad to get back within the borders of civilization. Coolgardie is three yards inside of it; Perth is about a mile, and of course San Francisco is the center. Anybody who envies me my salary can just take my next trip with me, and he will then be contented to be a bank clerk at $3 a week for the rest of his life, just to live in the United States. Stanford is the best place in the world."[2]

Not surprisingly, Hoover acquired a nickname in Australia. H. C. were the initials of his first and middle names: H. C. Hoover. His friends said that H. C. stood for "Hail Columbia."

Hoover's success in the land down under was immediate. Before he was twenty-four he was made superintendent of what became one of the greatest gold mines in Australian history. Then, late in 1898, his British employer offered him an even better job in China. Before going there, he returned to California and married his sweetheart, Lou Henry (Stanford, class of 1898). The very next day they boarded a ship for China, where they lived for more than two years and survived a harrowing brush with death in the Boxer Rebellion. Once again Hoover, a go-getting American still in his twenties, found himself living among strangers and encountering a foreign civilization.

In late 1901, Hoover left China for England and a partnership in the firm of mining engineers that had hired him less than five years before. Until World War I, London, the mining and financial capital of the world, was his base of operations while he traveled continually, inspecting, financing, and developing mines from Burma to Australia, from South Africa to Siberia. By 1914 he had traveled around the world five times and had mining interests on every continent except Antarctica.

For some Americans with similar careers and lifestyles, the temptation might have been irresistible to become an expatriate. For Hoover the very opposite was true. In London, his pro-American sentiments were so pronounced that he was known to some as the "star-spangled Hoover." Throughout these "years of adventure," as he called them, his thoughts often turned back to his native land, where he planned eventually to resettle.

And all the while, in England and on his many business journeys, he was observing and evaluating the social systems of the Old World and the New. On one of his ocean voyages, a British lady asked him what his profession was. An engineer, he replied. "Why," she exclaimed, "I thought you were a gentleman!" This anecdote, which Hoover later recounted in his memoirs, epitomized his deep distaste for the class consciousness and social rigidities of Europe.[3] From all of this he turned.

In 1914, World War I enveloped Europe and utterly changed the course of Hoover's life. While giant European armies bogged down in the trenches, Hoover, working without pay, founded and directed the Commission for Relief in Belgium (CRB), a neutral organization that procured and distributed food to the entire civilian population of Belgium caught between a German army of occupation and a British naval blockade. It was an unprecedented undertaking that eventually brought food to more than nine million people a day and catapulted Hoover to worldwide fame as a humanitarian.

When the United States entered the war in 1917, Hoover left day-to-day administration of the CRB to neutral subordinates and returned home to America, where he became head of the United States Food Administration, a special wartime agency of the federal government. At the end of the conflict in November 1918, President Woodrow Wilson sent him back across the Atlantic, this time to feed starving Europe and facilitate its economic reconstruction, while Wilson and Allied leaders struggled to draft a peace treaty in Paris. As director general of the American Relief Administration, Hoover organized the supply of food to suffering people in more than twenty nations, in the process helping to check the advance of Communist revolution from the east. Tens of millions of people owed their lives to his exertions. It was later said of him that he was responsible for saving more lives than any other person in history.

On September 13, 1919, the international humanitarian hero returned at last to America's shores. Despite his phenomenal accomplishments in the preceding ten months, he was not a contented man. Every day at the peace conference in Paris, he had witnessed a depressing display of national rivalries, vengefulness, and greed. He had seen, as well, the sometimes violent attempts by Communists and other radicals to construct a new social order in Europe on the principles of Marxist socialism. And increasingly he had viewed America in contrast.

Hoover returned to his native land with two dominant convictions. The first was that the ideology of socialism, as tested before his very eyes in Europe, was a catastrophic failure, unable to motivate men and women to produce sufficient goods for the needs of society. Hoover's second conviction was also firmly held. More than ever before, he sensed the "enormous distance" that America had drifted from Europe in its 150 years of nationhood, a distance reflected, he said, in "our outlook on life, our relations toward our neighbors and our social and political ideals."[4] Coming back to the United States from Europe, Hoover sensed that his own country was vulnerable to the afflictions he had witnessed abroad. He implored his fellow citizens not to turn their country into "a laboratory for experiment in foreign social diseases."[5]

In numerous speeches and articles Hoover began to define the American alternative. The foundation of the distinctive American social philosophy, he asserted, was the principle of *equality of opportunity*—the idea that no one should be "handicapped in securing that particular niche in the community to which his abilities and character entitle him." Unlike Europe, where oppressive class barriers had generated misery and revolutionary discontent, the American social system was

based, in his words, upon the "negation of class."[6] To Hoover the principle of equality of opportunity was quite simply "our most precious social
ideal."[7] As he put it some years later, "This idea of a fluid classless society
was unique in the world. It was the point at which our social structure
departed from all others."[8]

In the 1920s and later, Hoover continued to ask himself: Why is
America so different? Why is it unique? One result of his inquiry into
this issue was a little volume called *American Individualism,* which he
published in 1922. In it, he articulated America's bedrock social philosophy of cooperative individualism, in contrast to the pernicious collec-
tivistic competitors that were bubbling up overseas.

Another result of his ruminations was a book of political philosophy titled *The Challenge to Liberty,* which appeared in 1934, after he
left the White House. It was a powerful defense of what he now called
"Historic Liberalism" against the ascendant statist ideologies of Europe,
including fascism, Nazism, and communism—and against the American variant of statism, which he called "Regimentation," his term for
Franklin Roosevelt's New Deal.

In 1919 and 1920, Hoover's vexation with Europe had not been so
deep as to preclude his advocacy of American involvement in European
affairs. But as the years passed, his estrangement from Europe gradually intensified. The New World, he came to believe, was remote from
the fanatic ideologies, ethnic animosities, dictatorships, power politics,
imperialism, and class stratification of Europe. What he had witnessed
in 1919, he concluded, was something far more profound than "the
intrigues of diplomacy or the foibles of European statesmen." It was "the
collision of civilizations that had grown three hundred years apart."[9]

These outspoken sentiments undergirded Hoover's opposition between 1939 and 1941 to American entry into World War II before Pearl
Harbor. They also colored his attitude toward US foreign aid to Europe in the late 1940s and toward American military strategy during
the Cold War. His knowledge of European history and social injustices

made him leery of American interventionism abroad. It was America's "national mission," he said in 1938, "to keep alight the lamp of true liberalism." And, he added, it was "in the United States that we must keep it alight."[10]

It is unusual for American presidents to venture self-consciously into the realm of political philosophy; Herbert Hoover did. Unlike most American men of affairs, who have been content to act on the public stage but not to meditate much about it, he endeavored to explain the essence of the American regime he cherished.

Why? The fundamental reason, I believe, is this: more than any other man who has held the office of the presidency, Hoover was profoundly acquainted over an extended period with the ruling elites and social systems of the Old World. "I have seen the squalor of Asia, the frozen class barriers of Europe. And I was not a tourist," he said on one occasion.[11] He had seen the haughty oligarchies of the Right, the bloody tyrannies of the Left, and the hatreds, injustices, and miseries they engendered. He had seen the terrible consequences of imperialism, war, and revolution as few Americans ever had.

"My every frequent homecoming," he declared in 1948, "has been a reaffirmation of the glory of America. Each time my soul was washed by the relief from grinding poverty of other nations, by the greater kindliness and frankness which comes from the acceptance of equality and a belief in wide-open opportunity to all who want a chance. It is more than that. It is a land of self-respect born alone of free men and women."[12]

This perception of contrast between the Old World and the New was the experiential core of Hoover's social and political philosophy. It gave him a lifelong understanding of America as an exceptionally free, humane, and classless society that had come closer to implementing its ideals than any other nation on earth. It gave him a fervent sense of American uniqueness, a conviction that the United States was, in his words, "one of the last few strongholds of human freedom." It impelled him to undertake, in his postpresidential years, what he called a "crusade against collectivism": a crusade to preserve the American system of liberty from enemies both foreign and domestic.

Hoover labeled his core value system "American Individualism" and, later on, "Historic Liberalism." For us today, a comparable term would be "American exceptionalism." But whatever the label, Hoover taught us something we might well ponder: that in an epoch of wars and revolutions it is political philosophy, however perverted, that moves men and women for good or ill.

From a lifetime of comparative social analysis, Hoover derived this lesson: that in the lives and destinies of nations, ideas—and ideals—have mattered. And I think he would say they still do.

Notes

1. Herbert Hoover, *Years of Adventure, 1874–1920,* vol. 1 of *The Memoirs of Herbert Hoover* (New York: Macmillan, 1951), 30.
2. Herbert Hoover to Harriette Miles, August 5, 1897, extracted in "Mining—Australia, Herbert Hoover's Account of Western Australia," Pre-Commerce Papers, Herbert Hoover Papers, Herbert Hoover Presidential Library, West Branch, Iowa.
3. Hoover, *Years of Adventure,* 132.
4. Herbert Hoover, "The Safety of New-born Democracies," *Forum* 62 (December 1919): 551.
5. Ibid., 561.
6. Herbert Hoover, inaugural address (American Institute of Mining and Metallurgical Engineers [AIMME], February 17, 1920), Public Statements File, Herbert Hoover Papers, Herbert Hoover Presidential Library, West Branch, Iowa.
7. Herbert Hoover, commencement address (William Penn College, Oskaloosa, Iowa, June 12, 1925), printed in *Penn College Bulletin,* n.s., 19 (July 1925).
8. Herbert Hoover, *Further Addresses upon the American Road, 1938–1940* (New York: Scribner's, 1940), 221.
9. Hoover, *Years of Adventure,* 479.
10. Herbert Hoover, *Addresses upon the American Road, 1933–1938* (New York: Scribner's, 1938), 322.
11. Herbert Hoover, *Addresses upon the American Road, 1945–1948* (New York: Scribner's, 1949), 77.
12. Ibid.

Ronald Reagan and American Exceptionalism

ANNELISE ANDERSON

Ronald Reagan's earliest explicit view of American exceptionalism was expressed in a speech he gave to the 1952 graduating class at William Woods College in Fulton, Missouri, the same town in which Winston Churchill had told the United States that an iron curtain had fallen across Europe from Stettin in the Baltic to Trieste in the Adriatic. At this time Reagan had been out of the country on only one occasion, when he had gone to England to make a movie. He hadn't liked England—the food was not good, the people were regimented, and it was too cold.

At the time he spoke at William Woods College, he had nowhere near Herbert Hoover's international experience. He had served in World War II, making training films for the Army Air Corps, at which time he had already made thirty feature films. After the war he returned to his acting career and became president of the Screen Actors Guild, where he negotiated with studio heads on behalf of actors and fought attempts by Communist-infiltrated unions to take over Hollywood. By 1952 he was not getting very good roles. He had married his second wife,

Nancy Davis, a few months before, and his job representing General Electric, which would make him a prominent television personality, was two years in the future.

This is what he said to the graduating seniors: "I, in my own mind, have thought of America as a place in the divine scheme of things that was set aside as a promised land. . . . Any person with the courage, with the desire to tear up their roots, to strive for freedom, to attempt and dare to live in a strange and foreign place, was welcome here."[1] As he often said, this was a place people could come to be free and to become Americans, a place founded on an idea rather than an ethnic heritage, religion, or race. Lou Cannon, Reagan's main biographer, points out that Reagan held this view throughout his life and that it never degenerated into a view of American superiority.

Reagan's view of American exceptionalism is often summarized in a phrase that turns up in many of his speeches—a "city on a hill." When he uses this phrase, he's quoting John Winthrop speaking to the pilgrims on the deck of the *Arbella* off the coast of Massachusetts in 1630. But the full quote, which Reagan used in a 1978 radio commentary written in his own hand in the years between his governorship of California and the presidency, emphasizes that because this city is on a hill, it is open to the judgment of others: "We shall be as a city on a hill," Winthrop says. "The eyes of all people are upon us, so that if we shall deal falsely with our God in this work we have undertaken and so cause him to withdraw his present help from us, we shall be made a story and a byword throughout the world."[2]

In 1980, when Ronald Reagan was elected president of the United States, the concept of American exceptionalism was being challenged. People were periodically waiting in lines to buy gasoline. The economy was in trouble: both unemployment and inflation were high, and growth was slow. It was called "stagflation." The consumer price index, mortgage rates, the prime lending rate—all were in double digits. Hostages had been held in the American embassy in Iran for over a year.

Worst of all, the country seemed to have lost confidence in its future and its position in the world. An attempt to rescue the Iranian hostages failed. President Jimmy Carter had tried to negotiate with the Soviets on arms control and finally realized, when they invaded Afghanistan in December 1979, that their intentions were not as benign as he had believed. The Soviet invasion of Afghanistan postponed indefinitely the Senate's consideration of the second Strategic Arms Limitation Talks treaty.

The general view in the community of academics and pundits was that the Soviet Union was a permanent opponent of the United States, one with whom we needed to coexist indefinitely. Many people thought the economic and political systems of the two superpowers were converging, becoming more like one another. Some of the experts—including experts prominent in the Nixon and Ford administrations—doubted that a political system based on individual freedom and free markets could compete effectively with a centrally controlled economy that could extract resources from its citizenry at will and could override and repress political dissent.

Reagan had no such doubts. He had confidence in the American system and its capability to compete with communism, and he set out immediately upon becoming president to restore the US economy and to persuade the Soviet Union—through an arms buildup—that they could not compete with the United States and that therefore arms reduction—rather than an arms buildup—was in their best interest.

An important part of Reagan's view of American exceptionalism was a rejection of the view that the United States and the Soviets were two apes on a treadmill—that the two systems were different but morally equivalent. It was the American system that freed the individual genius of people and gave people dignity.

Reagan gave many speeches that expressed these ideas, but some of my favorite quotations are those that are the least scripted, where he got away from the reviewers in the Department of State and even the

National Security Council and let the Soviets know what he thought of them.

He got right to it upon taking the presidency, in his first press conference, held January 29, 1981. Reagan noted that day that the Soviets have often repeated that their goal is world revolution and a one-world communist state and that they considered to be moral anything they did to attain that goal. The United States operated, he continued, on a different set of standards. Reagan's statement was his first explicit rejection as president of the idea of moral equivalence between the United States and the Soviet Union, and it shocked the press and the world. Here are his specific words:

> I know of no leader of the Soviet Union since the revolution, and including the present leadership, that has not more than once repeated in the various Communist congresses they hold their determination that their goal must be the promotion of world revolution and a one-world Socialist or Communist state. . . . They have openly and publicly declared that the only morality they recognize is what will further their cause, meaning they reserve unto themselves the right to commit any crime, to lie, to cheat, in order to attain that, and that is moral, not immoral, and we operate on a different set of standards. I think when you do business with them, even at a detente, you keep that in mind.[3]

An important expression of Reagan's views came in his June 1982 speech to the British Parliament in which he talks about "a plan and a hope for the long term—the march of freedom and democracy which will leave Marxism-Leninism on the ash-heap of history as it has left other tyrannies which stifle the freedom and muzzle the self-expression of the people."[4] But Reagan also talks in this speech about self-determination and fostering the infrastructure of democracy. He does not claim, as President George W. Bush did in his second inaugural address, that democracy in other countries was essential to our own security or that we would base our relations with other countries on our judgment of how they treated their people.

Reagan gave a speech in March 1983 in which he emphasized the moral distinction between the United States and the Soviet Union. In this speech he called the Soviet Union "the focus of evil in the modern world"[5]—a line he wrote himself. It was a speech to the National Association of Evangelicals in Orlando, Florida, in which he encouraged them to take sides on the question of putting nuclear weapons in Europe to oppose those that the Soviets already had in place, aimed at Western capitals. The speech was not widely reviewed in advance in the channels of the US government. In fact, Nancy wanted him to soften it, but he refused, telling her that he wanted the Soviets to know what he thought of them. It was a decision made with full intent.

Reagan's speech in 1987 at the Brandenburg Gate, on the western side of the Berlin Wall, was another such speech. This one did go through the full review process, and Reagan had to fight to keep the now-famous phrase "Tear down this wall." He challenged Mikhail Gorbachev, in the name of peace and prosperity, to open the gate and tear down the wall.

In conclusion, Reagan's personal view was that America was a special place where people could come to be free—a place chosen by God but also accountable—a city on a hill, visible to all, where all could come to be free and become American. Obviously one cannot view Reagan's vision without also asking about his immigration policy. Reagan's campaign for the presidency in 1980 included the idea of a North American accord to improve relations among the nations of Mexico, Canada, and the United States. The idea of closer relationships among the nations on the North American continent eventually resulted in the North American Free Trade Agreement, under challenge in the presidential election of 2016. Immigration was an issue in the 1980 campaign, partly because of the Mariel boatlift, in which Fidel Castro permitted close to 125,000 Cubans to leave the island nation on boats bound for the United States.

Mexico at that time was a third-world country bordering a first-world country, and the border was a long one. Many people crossed that border for temporary or permanent work, and many of these lived in the United States without having been legally admitted. The birthrate in Mexico was very high at the time. That has changed in recent years; the birthrate has fallen, and there has been little if any net migration from Mexico to the United States according to recent statistics. But it was a problem at that time, and I'd like to end by quoting a comment Reagan made in April 1980 during a debate with George H. W. Bush, his remaining opponent for the 1980 Republican presidential nomination:[6]

> I think the time has come that the United States and our neighbors, particularly our neighbor to the south, should have a better understanding and a better relationship than we've ever had, and I think we haven't been sensitive to our size and our power. They have a problem of 40 to 50 percent unemployment. Now this cannot continue without the possibility arising with regard to that other country that we talked about, of Cuba and everything it is stirring up, of the possibility of trouble below the border, and we could have a very hostile and strange neighbor on our border.
>
> Rather than making them or talking about putting up a fence, why don't we work out some recognition of our mutual problems, make it possible for them to come here legally with a work permit, and then, while they're working and earning here, they pay taxes here? When they want to go back, they can go back and they can cross and open the border both ways. By understanding their problems—this is the only safety valve they have right now, with that unemployment, that probably keeps the lid from blowing off down there. I think we could have a fine relationship.

Notes

1. Ronald Reagan, "America the Beautiful: Commencement Address" (William Woods College, Fulton, Missouri, June 2, 1952), printed in *Echoes in the Woods* 39, no. 2.2: 8–13. Copy in vertical file at the Ronald Reagan Presidential Library.

2. Ronald Reagan, "Two Worlds," August 7, 1978, printed in *Reagan, in His Own Hand,* ed. Kiron K. Skinner, Annelise Anderson, and Martin Anderson (New York: Free Press, 2001), 14.

3. Ronald Reagan, "The President's News Conference" (January 29, 1981), https://reaganlibrary.archives.gov/archives/speeches/1981/12981b.htm (accessed June 1, 2017).

4. Ronald Reagan, "Address to the Members of the British Parliament" (June 8, 1982), quoted in *Reagan's Secret War: The Untold Story of His Fight to Save the World from Nuclear Disaster,* ed. Martin Anderson and Annelise Anderson (New York: Crown, 2009), 253–54.

5. Ronald Reagan, "Remarks at the Annual Convention of the National Association of Evangelicals" (Orlando, Florida, March 8, 1983), quoted in *Reagan's Secret War* (see note 4), 122.

6. "Republican Debate between Reagan and Bush," April 24, 1980, YouTube, https://youtube.com/watch?v=YfHN5QKq9hQ (accessed June 1, 2017).

The American Dream Is Alive in the Minds of Young Americans

WILLIAM DAMON

Other presentations in this volume have discussed important features of American exceptionalism from economic, historical, legal, and policy perspectives. I have no expertise in those fields, and I have learned a great deal from the authors of presentations that draw on them.

My own field of study is psychology. As a psychologist, I am interested in people's beliefs and in how their beliefs influence the choices that shape their lives. From my perspective as a psychologist, the emblematic symbol of American exceptionalism is a belief in what has been called "the American dream." This is a belief that has fostered hope, accomplishment, and success for generations of Americans, and it has been an aspirational goal for millions of young people throughout history.

Where did the idea of the American dream come from? The general notion most likely evolved early in our nation's history, as legions of Americans became aware of the freedoms and opportunities that had made their own advancement possible. But the actual term itself was coined by historian James Truslow Adams in a 1931 book called *The Epic of America*. The way Adams defined it, the American dream is "that dream of a land in which life should be better and richer for everyone, with opportunities for each according to ability and achievement. . . . It is not a dream of high wages or motorcars merely. It is a dream of social order in which each man and each woman shall be able to attain to the fullest stature."

What is notable in Adams's definition is that the American dream is not an entitlement, something that you are given, something you're guaranteed, but it's an opportunity that you have. Ability and achievement are determining factors. Adams also points out that material success is one important part of the American dream but not the only part. He put the word "merely" after "high wages" and "motorcars" because, yes, material aspiration is a healthy ambition, but it takes its place among broader aspects of attainment, including social and spiritual attainment, in a social order that allows people to reach their "fullest stature" in every sense. Conceived in this way, the American dream stands as one of the truly noble—and exceptional—standards of world history.

Yet a surprising bit of information that I'll mention is that the American dream is far from an accepted notion in our country today. There is a widespread view that the American dream is a myth or that it is dying. In fact, if you google the phrase "*death* of the American dream," you will get somewhere around thirty-four million hits. Now I'm not implying that each hit is unique, and the Google algorithm doesn't exactly produce reliable data. But I do think that this is a fair indicator that there is a lot of skepticism these days about the reality and viability of the American dream. This skepticism is prevalent in media, books, articles, in what academics write in journals, and in what leading social commentators are writing. It is clear from all these sources—all of which are picked up by the Google search—that the idea of the American dream is not in high repute in our public discourse at the present time.

For example, one distinguished professor has written that the American dream is "the dream that this country is a place where anybody who builds a better mousetrap can get rich."[1] This is a sardonic comment about one component of the American dream, and it ignores its more evocative components, such as the promise of living a fulfilling life by freely following the voice of one's own conscience. Others who have recently written about the American dream go even further toward a materialistic reduction by linking it to specific consumer attainments, such as home ownership and the two-car garage.[2]

When critics ground their views in a wholly material interpretation of the American dream, they dismiss its authenticity. One popular book along these lines bears the subtitle *The Futile Pursuit of the American Dream*—a characterization largely in keeping with the consensus of critical intellectual thinking on the matter.[3] Such views reduce the elevated notion that Adams formulated into trivial terms that express cynicism in the way these writers have phrased them. In such views, which influence the media and account for the millions of Google hits I noted, the American dream has been diminished to no more than an idea of gaining celebrity and getting rich quick.

The question that I will explore here is, what do young people in our country believe about the American dream? Do their beliefs reflect the cynicism present in our public discourse, or do they match the more elevated vision described by James Truslow Adams?

The research institution at Stanford that I direct, the Stanford Center on Adolescence, examines how people acquire and develop their beliefs. Our center's primary interest in recent years has been how people find their purposes in life. Ours is a small research center that focuses mainly on younger people; but in the special case of purpose, we have looked at many ages, even as late as retirement age (in collaboration with the non-profit group Encore.org and the Stanford Distinguished Careers Institute recently launched by former Stanford School of Medicine dean Dr. Philip Pizzo). In our research with young people in the adolescent and young adult age groups, our particular interest has been in how they find the purposes that will direct their lives in the future. What motivates these young people? What do they find meaningful? What leads them to strive, to achieve, to become the kinds of people that they most want to become? We examine many areas of young people's lives. We are interested in academic motivation, the motivation to acquire a fulfilling career, the motivation to build a family life, and the motivation to contribute positively to their communities.

Our center's research director, Heather Malin, working with several of our graduate student research assistants, conducted a study a few years ago to explore the question of what American citizenship means to the young people in our country. In this study, Dr. Malin and her research team interviewed young people about what it means to be an American these days. I'll quote from these interviews, letting the voices of the young people speak for themselves. I'll also identify in the quotes some themes that I would like to point out about how the American dream is viewed by young Americans today—the hopes and beliefs that were typical in the population of young people that Dr. Malin and her research team spoke with. These themes were typical of the sample as a whole. I haven't selected unusual types of quotes. My overall conclusion is that, for a great many young people today, the American dream is alive and well.

"I hear 'American dream,' and I think the chance to pursue your dreams, the daring to be whoever you want to be. . . . Well, I guess it inspires me."

In talking about the meaning of the American dream, this girl highlights the idea of having a *chance*. We will see that a lot in these quotes. This girl says very directly, "It inspires me." These young people don't all use the exact term "inspire," but you will hear a sense of inspiration in all of the quotes.

"To me, personally, it's really the right to live a life the way you want to live, the right to prosper. It's basically . . . having a chance to start a life,

start a living, raise a family, do whatever you want as long as it's under the law. I think it's really meaningful, and that's another reason why I love this country."

Again, the American dream is not a trivial concept to these young folks. It's meaningful. It inspires them.

"The American dream is just basically the chance to succeed, the promise and the hope of something better being out there . . . a road that will lead me to a better step. Not necessarily even more money, because money's not a huge deciding factor in my career choice, but it's kind of more like the pursuit of happiness."

Note that this boy says "the chance to succeed," "the promise and hope of something better being out there." None of these young people are speaking of a guarantee, of some sort of *entitlement* to succeed. We don't see that in these interviews. We see a focus on *opportunity,* an appreciation of having a shot at success. This boy said something that also runs throughout the interviews: it's "not necessarily even more money." Now, of course, the American dream has a large material aspect to it; and many of these young people recognize that material success is important, but a lot of them emphasized that this is not the only thing. That's a point that I'm going to return to later.

"It's a chance of pursuit of happiness."

That sounds a bit like the Declaration of Independence.

"Nevertheless, despite the problems, there's still a lot of opportunity out there."

This boy also talked about freedom and having a voice in government and, again, opportunities. He mentions some problems in the country. Not all of these young people were uncritical about every aspect of our country, but they usually returned to the idea that their perceptions of these problems do not defuse the opportunity that they see.

"The American dream is the ability through hard work and determination to rise. It is the right to be given the opportunities to do as you will. It is *the right to choose for yourself, and that's what I feel the American dream is. . . . I think it plays a role mainly in values, but also in the way I act and the way I plan to act."*

This boy is determined to take advantage of the opportunity this country offers "through hard work and determination," the need for which is a realization that many young people have, despite views to the contrary. That actually surprised me a bit because we may not often think of young people as fully endorsing the fact you have to work hard to deserve things and that life can be tough. But we saw this recognition throughout the interviews. The boy I quoted talked about values and "the way I act and the way I plan to act," which seems very impressive for an adolescent. In a follow-up interview, he said,

"It definitely means something. I'm just trying to figure out how best [to] define it because it means, in the end, so much. I think the American dream is the freedom to do as you will, and the ability to be rewarded for your work, to have a fair chance at success, whatever it means to you."

That quote shows that the boy was still grasping at this idea and trying to figure it out and decide what it means to his life. In this way, the American dream can be a formative notion. It can be something that has influence on the direction of development of young people.

"I'm very fond of the American dream. The American dream to me pretty much means freedom. It means that it doesn't matter how wild your aspirations are; the American dream is to succeed in everything you've wanted to succeed in. If my dream is to become an astronaut, I'll become an astronaut."

That quote came from an eighteen-year-old with vaulting ambitions. When he says he is "very fond of the American dream," it means to him the freedom to aim high. It means aspirations that he mentions are "wild ones": becoming an astronaut, for example. It's about being able to choose what to do with one's life. He goes on to say,

"So the American dream to me, that aspiration . . . keeps me motivated, because it's not something where I'm going to get it handed to me. It's not

something that I'm going to receive by just sitting. It's something that I have to work for."

As I said earlier, the primary interest at our Center is what motivates young people to develop, to thrive, to succeed, and to strive, and this boy strongly associates the American dream with striving.

"The American dream to me personally is, to sum it up in one word, opportunity. Just to have the opportunity to be successful and to be happy in whatever way it makes you happy. . . . Everybody has their own little American dream. So just to look at my parents and see that they're still trying to live their American dream, still trying to provide for my siblings, it kind of hits me, [be]cause I kind of want the same things for my future family."

This boy talked about opportunity; the American dream means something to this boy and to his parents as well.

"[The American dream is] being able to be really poor and be able to, based on your own hard work, come up through the ranks. Being able to vote, exercise your rights, be able to say whatever you want and protest, have freedom to do your own religion, yes."

This girl mentions religion. This was another common theme. A lot of the young people talk about freedoms of speech and religion as essential features of the American dream.

"Those ideals definitely are an important part of my life. Freedom, because I feel like sometimes I may not have opinions that are popular with the majority, or have opinions that might ruffle some people's feathers. . . . It also helps me to feel like if I have the freedom to change . . . if we have the freedom to think differently, then we have the freedom to change."

This statement is especially interesting because this boy talks about the freedom to change himself, to grow in the way he wants to grow. Nobody's telling him what he must be in life—he can determine this for himself, according to the best guidance from his own conscience. Here's another boy speaking about freedom.

"I think the American dream is that people can be who they are. Like

freedom of religion, freedom of speech, freedom of action and stuff. I believe in that. People can be who they want to be."

Finally there was a theme across some of the interviews about being able to live in peace, similar to James Truslow Adams's ideas of having a social order that you can trust. One boy put it this way:

"The way I see the American dream is being able to live in peace, meaning you don't have to worry. . . . It's not being rich, it's not being rolling in money. . . . It's like the land of the free, so you basically have opportunities and open doors for a better life."

In the following quote, a girl talks about security, safety, equal opportunity, equal rights, and how her parents succeeded through hard work.

"They go through all the struggle, so that their children have a better life. . . . They have an equal opportunity and equal rights, but not equality in everything. Equal opportunity. They have to work . . . but equal opportunity to pursue what they want. And security and safety. That'd be the American dream. . . . We're given that freedom to have all these dreams and these goals. . . . So in a way it's important to me just because it's not something we should take for granted."

The girl's statement that "it's not something we should take for granted" has special resonance for me. I will say that the sense of gratitude among virtually all of the young people I have quoted is very moving. I am a believer in gratitude as a virtue that promotes everything in life related to learning, open-mindedness, an appreciation for what you're receiving—including education; I always promote the idea of encouraging gratitude for schooling. Students who see schooling as a gift they are being offered, rather than as a burden put upon them, have a great advantage when it comes to motivation to learn. And any teacher will tell you that the key that unlocks the doors to learning is motivation.

The quotes that I have presented here suggest that when young Americans think about the meaning of the American dream, what they say is more in line with the elevated vision that James Truslow Adams formulated than with the degraded view promulgated in much of today's intellectual discourse and public media. I doubt that many young Americans have ever read Adams's formulation, but their views reflect a similar hopeful faith. Youth, of course, is a time of high idealism. This faith and idealism lends to a certain pride in the American tradition. Later in the interview, when we asked the question "Are you proud to be an American?" we saw very much the same sense of why America is exceptional. For example, one girl said,

"We have the freedom to believe whatever we want. . . . We're blessed to have the opportunity to become anything we desire to be. That's a great advantage that we have in this country."

Again, we see gratitude arising from appreciation of America's exceptional promise.

It is noteworthy that pride, gratitude, and belief in the American dream among so many young Americans seem to be flourishing in the face of contrary media messages. Young people also confront similar contrary messages in some educational settings. Here is a quote from a high school senior from a study that we did some years ago:

"Last year the history teacher told us that the American dream was dead. I didn't believe that at all. The whole class was just sort of silent, and he could tell that we didn't really agree with that. If we didn't dream, then we wouldn't be doing anything. We wouldn't be advancing as a society."

This eighteen-year-old boy had a finer understanding of the American dream than his teacher; from what we can infer from his statement, so did his entire class. I worry what may happen to these eighteen-year-olds if they enter college and become exposed to even stronger negative opinions of the kind expressed by that high school teacher. Still, if the reaction of this boy's class is any indication, young Americans are not easily disabused of their hopes and dreams. One thing seems clear to me from the interviews I have quoted here: we have a large population of young people in this country who are full of optimism and high aspirations and who are grateful for the opportunities that our country offers them.

I'm going to close with one more bit of data. In our studies of purpose, we asked, "What's the very most important purpose that you have or that you see in your life?" The most common source of purpose that young people talk about is wanting to have a family and to support their families. Following right after that is work. Many want to have a great career. They want to learn a lot to build their prospects. For a smaller but stable portion of the youth population, their most important purpose is to devote themselves to their faith and serve God. These are all fine purposes. But only a very few of the young people we interviewed expressed aspirations to serve as a civic leader of some kind—city council member, school board member, town mayor, and so on.

I believe that more young people would become interested in this kind of civic leadership if they learned more from their history courses about sacrifices that previous generations of great Americans made to secure the benefits of the American dream for those to come. As several of the Founding Fathers warned, freedom requires sacrifice. A call to sacrifice, a call to dedicate themselves to a noble cause, is exactly what young people need. They do not need to be told, "Don't worry. We're going to do everything for you. We're going to protect you. We're going to provide money and security and all the things you need without your having to do anything." That is not what brings out the best in young people. They want to be called on to chip in. They want to think that their lives matter, that they can make a difference. The idea that service to the country is a noble cause is an idea that many generations have shared. There are a lot of people in the history of our country who have sacrificed and given us the great blessings that we have. We don't want to just be nostalgic in our thinking about the "greatest generation" and so on. It's also very important that we have hopes for our children and our grandchildren to become great generations themselves and to do whatever is needed to secure the future of the country they will inherit. This is the mission that we older people can have: to pass along to the younger generation the mission of taking good care of this exceptional country that we're living in.

We have a good starting point. I've given you evidence of that. Young Americans today are eager to find purposes in life and to work toward achieving them. They've already figured out opportunities our country offers. These young Americans deserve our encouragement to maintain their optimistic beliefs about our future.

Notes

1. Christopher Jencks, "Reinventing the American Dream." *Chronicle of Higher Education*, October 17, 2008, B6.

2. William M. Rohe and Harry L. Watson, *Chasing the American Dream: New Perspectives on Affordable Homeownership* (Ithaca: Cornell University Press, 2007).

3. Barbara Ehrenreich, *Bait and Switch: The Futile Pursuit of the American Dream* (New York: Metropolitan Books, 2005).

ABOUT THE CONTRIBUTORS

GARY LIBECAP

Hoover Institution Research Fellow Gary D. Libecap is also the Distinguished Professor of Corporate Environmental Management at the Bren School of Environmental Science and Management and Distinguished Professor of Economics at the University of California, Santa Barbara. Libecap is an expert on property rights institutions: how they emerge and change and how they affect behavior and economic outcomes. Most of his research has focused on the problems of the common pool and how they are or are not effectively addressed.

VICTOR DAVIS HANSON

Victor Davis Hanson is the Martin and Illie Anderson Senior Fellow at the Hoover Institution and chairs Hoover's Working Group on the Role of Military History in Contemporary Conflict. His work focuses on classics and military history. He was awarded the National Humanities Medal in 2007 and the Bradley Prize in 2008. In 1992–93, Hanson was a National Endowment for the Humanities fellow at the Center for Advanced Studies in the Behavioral Sciences at Stanford University. He is the author of some twenty-four books on Greek, agrarian, and military history, as well as contemporary culture.

LEE OHANIAN

Hoover Institution Senior Fellow Lee E. Ohanian is also a professor of economics and director of the Ettinger Family Program in Macroeconomic

Research at the University of California, Los Angeles. He received his PhD from the University of Rochester. He is an adviser to the Federal Reserve Bank of Minneapolis and has previously advised a number of central banks in Europe. His research focuses on economic crises, economic growth, and the impact of public policy on the economy.

STEPHEN HABER

Stephen Haber is the Peter and Helen Bing Senior Fellow at the Hoover Institution and the A. A. and Jeanne Welch Milligan Professor in the School of Humanities and Sciences at Stanford University. In addition, he is a Stanford professor of political science, professor of history, and professor of economics (by courtesy), as well as a senior fellow of the Stanford Institute for Economic Policy Research. He is also the project director for Hoover's Working Group on Intellectual Property, Innovation, and Prosperity.

EDWARD P. LAZEAR

Edward P. Lazear is the Morris Arnold and Nona Jean Cox Senior Fellow at the Hoover Institution and the Davies Family Professor of Economics at the Stanford University Graduate School of Business. Lazear served in the White House from 2006 to 2009, where he was chairman of the President's Council of Economic Advisers.

MICHAEL McCONNELL

Hoover Institution Senior Fellow Michael W. McConnell is the Richard and Frances Mallery Professor and director of the Constitutional Law Center at Stanford Law School, as well as the codirector of Hoover's Regulation and Rule of Law Initiative. From 2002 to 2009 he served as a circuit judge on the United States Court of Appeals for the Tenth Circuit. Before his appointment to the bench, McConnell was the Presidential Professor at the S. J. Quinney College of Law at the University of Utah; before that he was the William B. Graham Professor of Law at the University of Chicago.

PAUL E. PETERSON

Hoover Institution Senior Fellow Paul E. Peterson is the senior editor of *Education Next: A Journal of Opinion and Research*. He is also the Henry Lee Shattuck Professor of Government and director of the Program on Education Policy and Governance at Harvard University. His research interests include educational policy, federalism, and urban policy. He has evaluated the effectiveness of school vouchers and other education reform initiatives.

WILLIAM DAMON

Hoover Institution Senior Fellow William Damon is also the director of the Stanford Center on Adolescence and a professor of education at Stanford University. Damon's research explores how people develop purpose in their work, family, and civic lives. He examines how young people can be educated to become devoted citizens and successful entrepreneurs and how older people can find new purposes later in life. Damon's work has been used in professional training programs in fields such as journalism, education, and business, as well as in character education programs in grades K–12. He is the author of the widely influential book *The Path to Purpose*. He has been elected to the National Academy of Education and the American Academy of Arts and Sciences.

JOHN COCHRANE

John H. Cochrane is a senior fellow at the Hoover Institution. He writes principally on monetary economics and finance, as well as macroeconomics, health insurance, time-series econometrics, financial regulation, and other topics. He is the author of the book *Asset Pricing*, was a coauthor of *The Squam Lake Report*, and recently created the Coursera online course Asset Pricing covering first-year PhD asset pricing material. Cochrane writes occasional op-eds, mostly in the *Wall Street Journal*, and blogs as *The Grumpy Economist* at johnhcochrane.blogspot.com. He is also a senior fellow at the Stanford Institute for Economic Policy Research, professor of finance and economics (by courtesy) at Stanford's Graduate School of Business, distinguished senior fellow at the University of Chicago Booth School of Business and the Becker-Friedman Institute, a research associate at the National Bureau of Economic Research, and an adjunct scholar at the Cato Institute. Cochrane's recent awards include the TIAA-CREF Institute Paul A. Samuelson Award for his book *Asset Pricing*, the Chookaszian Prize in Risk Management, the Faculty Excellence Award for MBA Teaching, and the McKinsey Award for Outstanding Teaching.

GEORGE H. NASH

George H. Nash is a historian, lecturer, and authority on the life of Herbert Hoover and the history of American conservatism. His publications include the first three volumes of a definitive, scholarly biography of Hoover and *The Conservative Intellectual Movement in America since 1945*. He has also edited two of Hoover's previously unseen memoirs: *Freedom Betrayed* and *The Crusade Years*. The holder of a PhD in history from Harvard University, Nash received the Richard M. Weaver Prize for Scholarly Letters in 2008.

KORI SCHAKE

Kori Schake is a research fellow at the Hoover Institution and a member of Hoover's Working Group on the Role of Military History in Contemporary Conflict. During the 2008 presidential election, she was senior policy adviser to the McCain-Palin campaign, responsible for policy development and outreach in the areas of foreign and defense policy. From 2007 to 2008 she was the deputy director for policy planning in the State Department. During President Bush's first term, she was the director for defense strategy and requirements on the National Security Council. She held the Distinguished Chair of International Security Studies at West Point and also served on the faculties of the Johns Hopkins School of Advanced International Studies, the University of Maryland's School of Public Affairs, and the National Defense University.

NIALL FERGUSON

Niall Ferguson, MA, D.Phil., is a Milbank Family Senior Fellow at the Hoover Institution, Stanford University, and a senior fellow at the Center for European Studies, Harvard, where he served for twelve years as the Laurence A. Tisch Professor of History. He is also a visiting professor at Tsinghua University, Beijing, and the Diller-von Furstenberg Family Foundation Distinguished Scholar at the Nitze School of Advanced International Studies in Washington, DC. He is the author of fourteen books, most recently *Kissinger, 1923–1968: The Idealist*, which won the Council on Foreign Relations Arthur Ross Prize. He is an award-making filmmaker, too, having won an international Emmy for his PBS series *The Ascent of Money*. His many other prizes include the Benjamin Franklin Prize for Public Service (2010), the Hayek Prize for Lifetime Achievement (2012), and the Ludwig Erhard Prize for Economic Journalism (2013).

ANNELISE ANDERSON

Annelise Anderson is a research fellow at the Hoover Institution. From 1981 to 1983, she was associate director for economics and government with the United States Office of Management and Budget.

Anderson coauthored *Ronald Reagan: Decisions of Greatness* (2015) and *Reagan's Secret War: The Untold Story of His Fight to Save the World from Nuclear Disaster* (2010) with Martin Anderson. She is also the coeditor of *Reagan, in His Own Hand* (2001) and *Reagan: A Life in Letters* (2003).

INDEX

Index

Department of Justice, US, (DOJ),
    25, 62–63
dismissal rate, 96
diversity, 118–19, 126
Dodd-Frank Act, 26, 28, 95, 97–98
DOJ. *See* Department of Justice, US

eBay, 42–43
economy, US, 57–58
    assessment of, 48
    growth of, early, 10–11
    intergenerational contract and, 79–80
    military budget and, 128
    mobility and, 48–49, 51–52, 53–54
    property rights and, 11, 41–42
    Reagan and, 144–45
    regulatory state and, 63
    Tocqueville on, 50
    US freedom and, 94–95, 99
    world leadership and, 54–55
    See also entrepreneurship; gross
        domestic product; income;
        labor force
education, in US, 12–13, 70
    geographic mobility and, 51
    mathematics proficiency in, 20n30,
        76–77, 96
    Middle Ages and, 124–25
    reform of, 86
    regulatory state criminalization
        and, 63
    about rule of law, 65
    unions and, 96
    in World University Rankings, 120
egalitarianism, 67, 74–75, 86
    See also equality
Ehrenreich, Barbara, 153
Eisenhower, Dwight, 69, 123
elections, 7, 8f, 17, 64–65
employment, 48, 52–53, 148
The End of History and the Last Man
    (Fukuyama), 106

Endangered Species Act, 33, 129
entitlement, 152, 155
entrepreneurship, 91, 93
    colonial Jamestown and, 89–90
    Democrats, taxes and, 96–97
    economic freedom and, 95, 99
    Great Recession and, 94
environmental regulation, 31–33, 34–35
The Epic of America (Adams, J. T.), 152
Epstein, Richard, 62
equality
    income, lack of, 10, 78, 79
    of opportunity, 138–39
Europe, 10, 19n11, 139–41
exceptionalism, American. *See specific
    topics*
executive branch, US, 25–26

favorability, of United States, 105–6
Federal Bureau of Investigation, US
    (FBI), 25
Federal Register, U.S., 80, 81f
federal systems, 73–74
federalism, 9, 128–29
"Federalist essay number 62"
    (Madison), 27
Ferguson, Niall, 79
fertility, 118, 125–26
feudal institutions, 6–7
financial regulatory sector, US, 26
Food Administration, US, 137
foreign policy, 69–70
    See also leadership; military, US
fossil fuels, 119, 126–27
    See also fracking
Founding Fathers, of United States,
    41, 58
    See also Adams, John; Boston Tea
        Party; Franklin, Benjamin;
        Jefferson, Thomas; Madison, James
fracking, 34–35, 37–38
Franklin, Benjamin, 18

Index